CAN'T
FIND
A
DRY
BALL

CAN'T FIND A DRY BALL

The Evansville Otters on the Lowest Rung of Baseball

Garret Mathews

ALBION PRESS

ALBION PRESS • TAMPA, FLORIDA

CAN'T FIND A DRY BALL
Copyright © 2002 by Garett mathews

All rights reserved. No part of this book may be reproduced without prior written permission from the publisher, except for brief excerpts to be used for review purposes.

ALBION PRESS
4532 West Kennedy Blvd., Suite 233
Tampa, FL 33609

Library of Congress Cataloging-in-Publication Data

Mathews, Garret.
   Can't find a dry ball : the Evansville Otters on the lowest rung of baseball / Garret Mathews.
     p. cm.
   ISBN 0-9709170-6-6
   1. Evansville Otters (Baseball team) 2. Minor league baseball—Indiana.
I. Title: Evansville Otters on the lowest rung of baseball. II. Title.
   GV875.E9 M38 2002
   796.357'64'09772—dc21
   2001008438

All photos by Denny Simmons (used with permission)
Text Design and composition by John Reinhardt Book Design

Printed in the United States of America

Contents

	Acknowledgments	vi
	Preface	vii
	Glossary	xi
1	Outta Your Head In the Bully	1
2	The Last Cut is the Deepest	21
3	Getting to Know You	41
4	I Went In Like It Was Death	61
5	The Far Eastern Connection, Cos and the Kite Man	81
6	The Dawn Patrol	105
7	A Brotherhood, Just Like the Elks	123
8	Leaving Is Such Sorrow	137
	Epilogue	153

I thank the Goldklang Group and the Bussing family, especially Bill, for their cooperation during the 2001 season.

I thank the skip, Dan Shwam. I snooped around more than a CIA agent and was the fifth wheel in his dugout for a ton of games, but the man never rang me up for being an interloper. He saw me mosey out to the bullpen night after night and not once suggested that wasn't the place for a 51-year-old.

Most of all, I thank the players:

Chris Adams. Jeremy Book. Billy Boughey. Don Blaylock. Rob Bowers. Cliff Brand. Todd Brown. Mike Butler. Louie Carmona. Jacob Chavez. Eric Cooper. Jeremy Coronado. Chris Cosbey. Gabriel Delgado.

Edwardo Fugueroa. Nolan Fry. Cliff Godwin. Joe Goodman. Travis Hardin. Steve Harris. Brian Harrison. Brad Hemmelgarn. Yasushi Hirose. Tomohiro Honda. Chris Howay. Josh Hudson. Joe Isaacson.

Keith Law. Brad Love. Craig Martin. Brandon Mattingly. Tom Miller. Yugi Nerei. Joe Nouguier. John Raffo. Alan Ready. B.J. Richter. Terry Roe. Mike Sabens.

Rob Skinnon. Jess Smith. Shane Smuin. Brad Steele. Nick Stelzner. Scott Suraci. Mark Thomas. Kevin Tracey. Alejandro Velazquez. Jewell Williams.

This book isn't about operating the Otters, or marketing the Otters, or leveraging the Otters.

It's about you guys.

What follows is my best rip.

I hope I got it right.

—G<small>ARRET</small> M<small>ATHEWS</small>

Preface

IALWAYS WANTED to follow a baseball team for a season. The intimacy of it. Dugout. Bullpen. Locker room. What the guys talk about when they're putting on their uniforms. What they say when they come back to the bench after hitting into a double play. How they react when the lineup card tells them someone else will be playing their position.

The grind of a season. How they're able to come to the park fresh when they've come to the park fresh 70 times already.

The relationships. Teammates they'd share a jockstrap with. Teammates they have nothing in common except the Y chromosome, but they join in the pile of bodies at home plate when the guy hits the game-winning bomb.

Baseball was the game I played the most as a child. Pitched to my brother with the screen door as a strike zone. Threw mile-high popups, or so I thought at the time, to neighbor kids under the street lights. Hit a 181-foot home run in Little League off Jason Harris, leading the Civitans to a 4-1 victory over the B&PW. It was the only jack of my career. Jason went on to star in science.

In high school, I ranged far to my right at second base (the distance increases exponentially every decade) and threw to first inches ahead of the runner to clinch the district championship, and at least somewhat make up for hitting so feebly that I was given the take sign with two strikes.

Baseball is the closest sport to my profession. Rain or shine, I write five columns a week for *The Evansville (Ind.) Courier & Press*. I've never missed a deadline.

A third baseman can hit for the cycle on Monday, the last line drive leaving a gash in the right-field fence. The manager tells the media he's got the stud of studs at the hot corner. But it doesn't mean squat when the guy steps on the field the next day. He has to do it all over again.

That's me with the column.

In our own way, we're each trying to go 5-for-5. The only difference is I don't have to worry about hitting the high hard one.

OK, so I wanted to hang around with a baseball team for a season.

Which team?

That was easy. The Evansville Otters of the independent Frontier League.

The team whose players share jockstraps not out of affection, but economic need. The team whose players would respond "bus" when asked their place of primary residence.

Real ballplayers, not the coddled kind you see on TV.

The sales pitch to lure them here sounded something like this:

"Hey, have we got just the deal for you. Come to Southern Indiana this summer and play ball in stifling heat and humidity for less money that the guy who scrapes caramel off the floor at the movieplex.

"You'll play in ripped pants and ride a dirty motor coach for what seems like forever, and when you finally get there, the room reservations will be all screwed up and you'll have to sit on the curb for two hours at 3 o'clock in the morning until it gets straightened out. How does being an Otter sound so far?

Great, huh. Wait, it gets better. You won't have a fancy apartment because you barely make enough to afford a welcome mat, and your chance of being picked up by an affiliated team is the same as throwing a spear through a nose ring. Like what you hear? Outstanding. See you May 18 for training camp."

A locker room full of guys from California to Georgia lovingly replied, "I do" to this job description and the 2001 season was on.

I was there, too, from the first fungo to Aug. 28 when the players inhaled the bus fumes for the last time.

There are hits and errors in this book. And games won and lost.

But that's only a semicolon of the story.

It's about getting to play and praying that the right people notice.

And not getting to play and dying a little every inning.

It's about seeing guys who have become close friends get released.

And wondering if the same fate is in store for you.

It's about the doubt whether you're good enough to play professional baseball.

And the sky-scraping joy when you find out you are.

It's about hoping a favorite teammate can come back from an arm injury.

And watching the enemy catcher take a foul tip in the privates, and making a sound like two pingpong balls going back and forth.

We talked during games, after games and at the motel, but probably our best chats came between 3 and 4 P.M. in the locker room when they were in transition between being just another 23-year-old guy with a backpack and an Otter. Here, they busted each other's chops, looked at their mail, swung their new bats and groused about somebody stealing their flip-flops.

It was a wonderful time.

I thought about it one night in the dugout when the moon was full and the stars looked like baby baseballs.

We'll never come this way again.

Them or me.

I'll assign my middle-aged self another book that doesn't involve protective cups.

The players will reintroduce themselves to their loved ones, and take up whatever it is in their lives that gives them the second-most enjoyment.

And, come next summer, they'll pray to God for a baseball uniform to put on.

I hope there is one for them.

If not, and with apologies to Paris, they can read this book and say, we'll always have Evansville.

Glossary

Blue — Umpire.
Bomb — Home run. Also jack.
Bully — Bullpen.
Bussie — Bus driver.
Cannon — Good arm.
Cheese — Fastball.
Clubbie — Clubhouse attendant. Someone who washes the players' uniforms and hangs them in the lockers.
Diesel — A large, strong individual. As in, "Who's that diesel playing third?"
Dirty — When a pitcher has good stuff. Also nasty.
Dose – From a pitcher's standpoint, to hit a batter with a pitch. As in, "My fingertips were sweating and I just knew I was going to dose the guy."
Grille — Mouth. As in, "That grounder took a bad hop and hit him in the grille."
Hit it with his purse — A bloop, excuse-me hit that barely gets over the infield.
Pimping it — When a hitter stands at the plate and enjoys his long home run too much to suit the opposition. Next time up, the guy can expect to get dosed.
Play Walt Disney — Act a part.
Pearls — Used baseballs that are in excellent condition.

Pipe — Strong throw across the diamond to get the runner at first. As in, "Hey, diesel, where'd you get that pipe?"

Piss-rod — Line drive.

Pole — In pre-game workouts, pitchers run from the right field foul pole to the one in left. The pitching coach varies the distance from day to day, but it is always measured in poles.

Rakes — Hits. Also rips. Also knocks. As in, "I had a great day at the plate. Got me three rakes."

She — A pitcher's arm. As in, "How is she today?"

Shut it down — No more base-stealing, because a team is winning by a significant margin and doesn't want to show up the opposition.

Slidepiece — Slider.

Snapdragon — Curveball.

Squeezed — A pitcher not getting the benefit of doubt on balls and strikes from the home plate umpire. As in, "Come on, blue, you're squeezing us."

Stat rat — Someone who pays too much attention to his individual performance.

Tank — Someone with a big ass.

Uni — Uniform.

Wear one — Let the pitch hit you.

PHOTO KEY

page 2—Thomas, Harrison; page 13—Brand; page 20—Smuin; page 40—Thomas; page 60—Brown, Shwam, Ryan; page 65—Figueroa; page 80—Cosbey; page 104—Figueroa, Delgado; page 111—Shwam, Carmichael; page 122—Mattingly; page 136—Becka Canterbury, Honda, Schwam; page 149—Brand; page 152—Nerei; pages 156-157—Evansville Otters

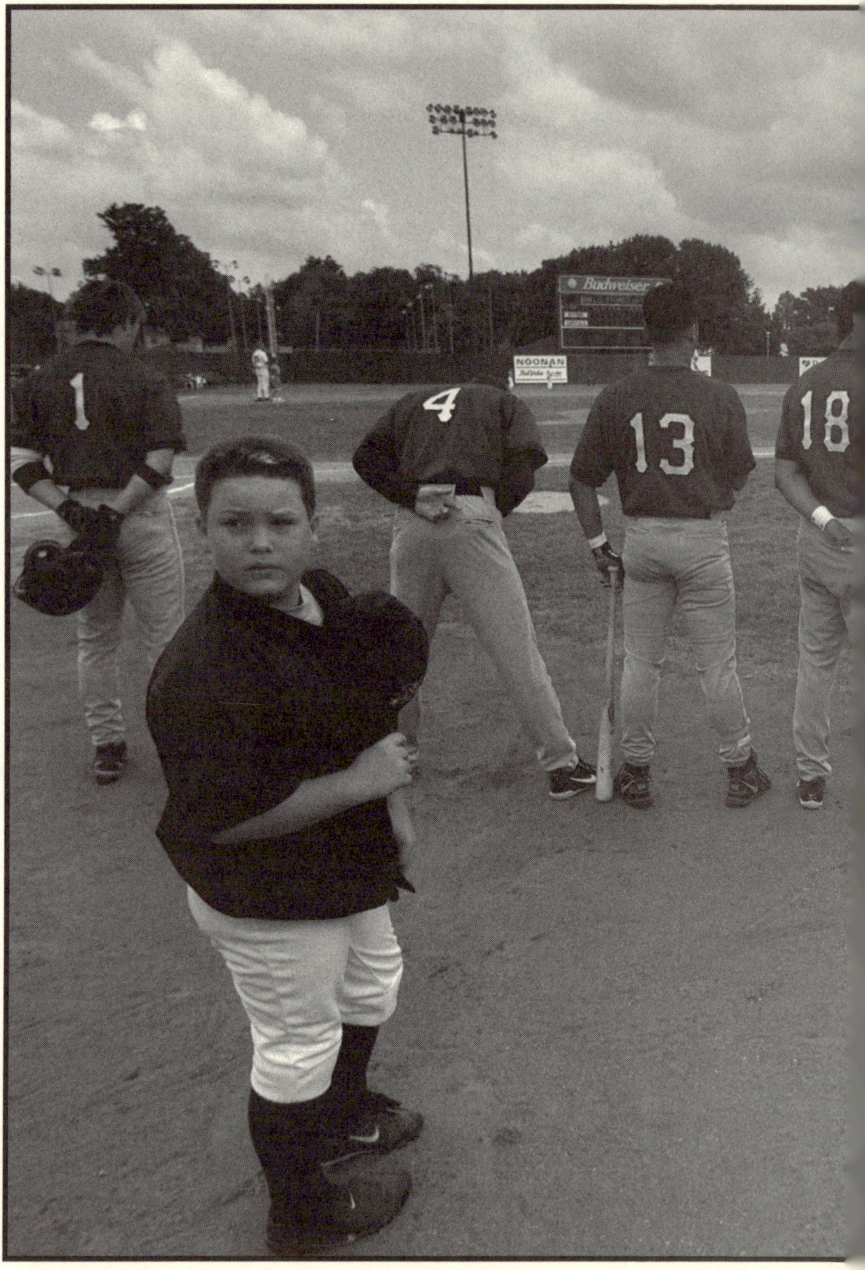
Budweiser
NOONAN
1
4
13
18

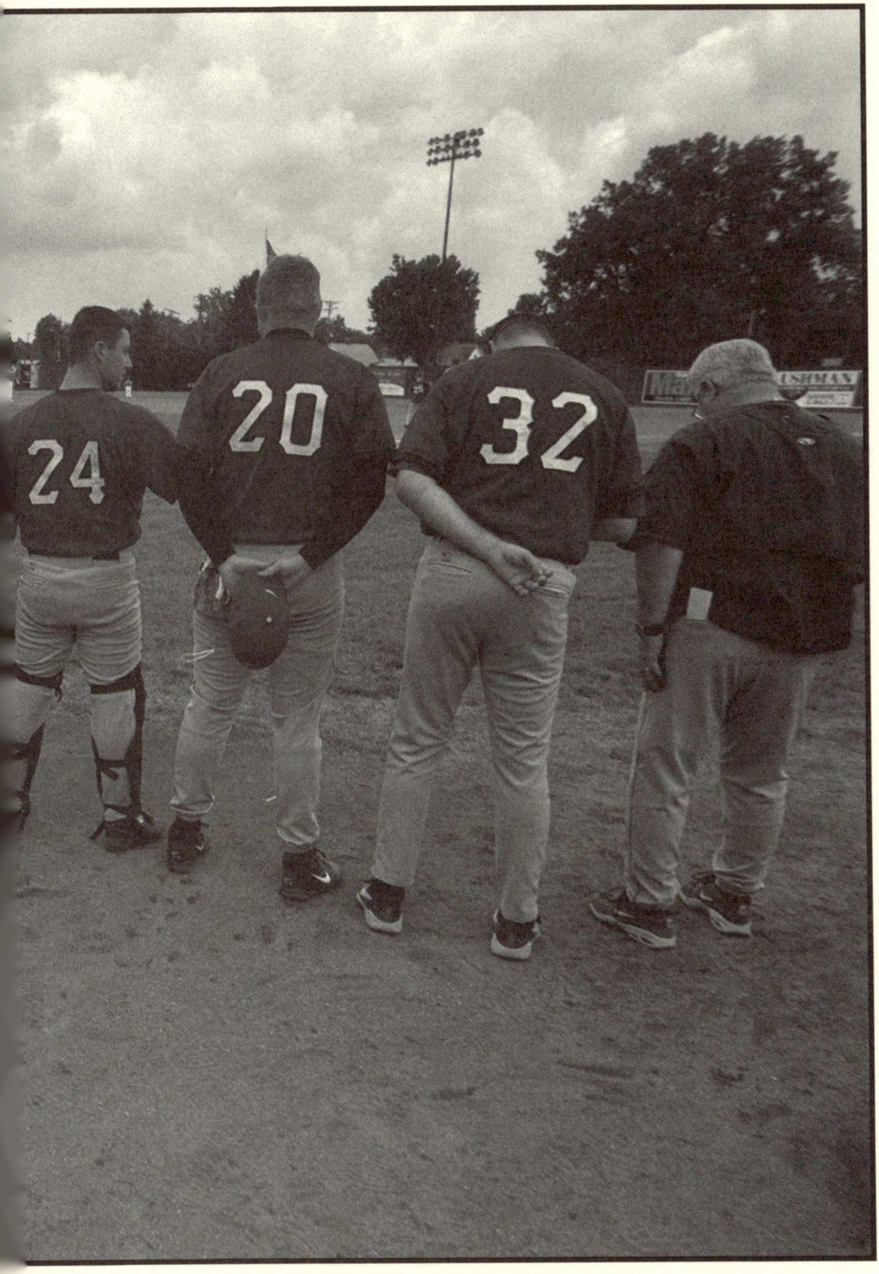
24
20
32

CAN'T
FIND
A
DRY
BALL

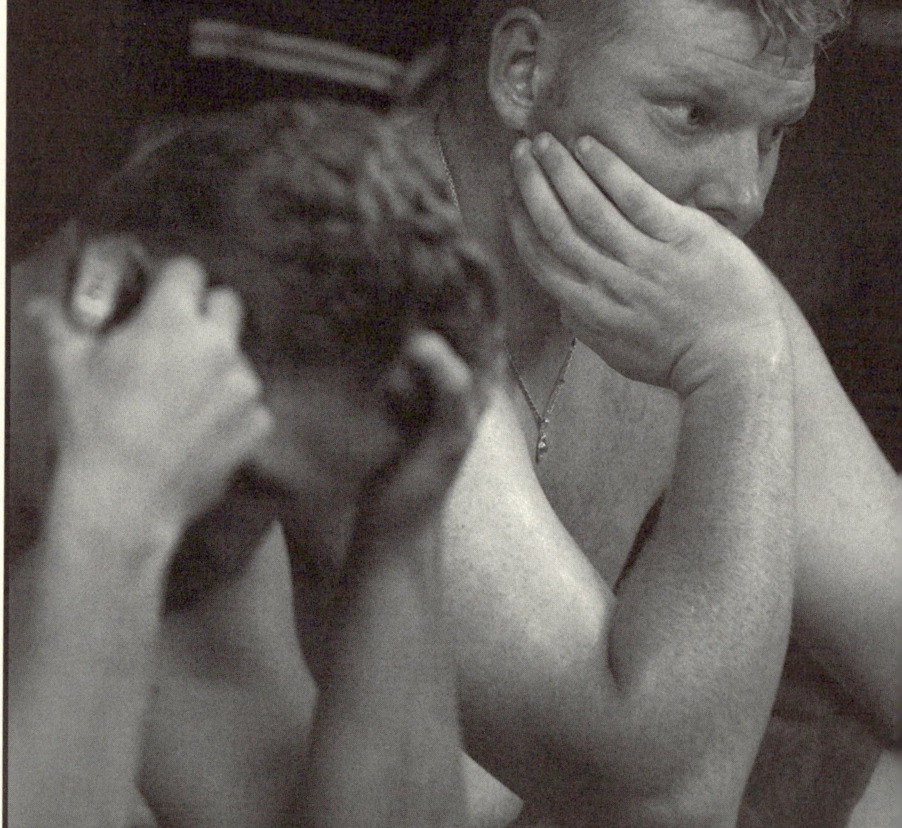

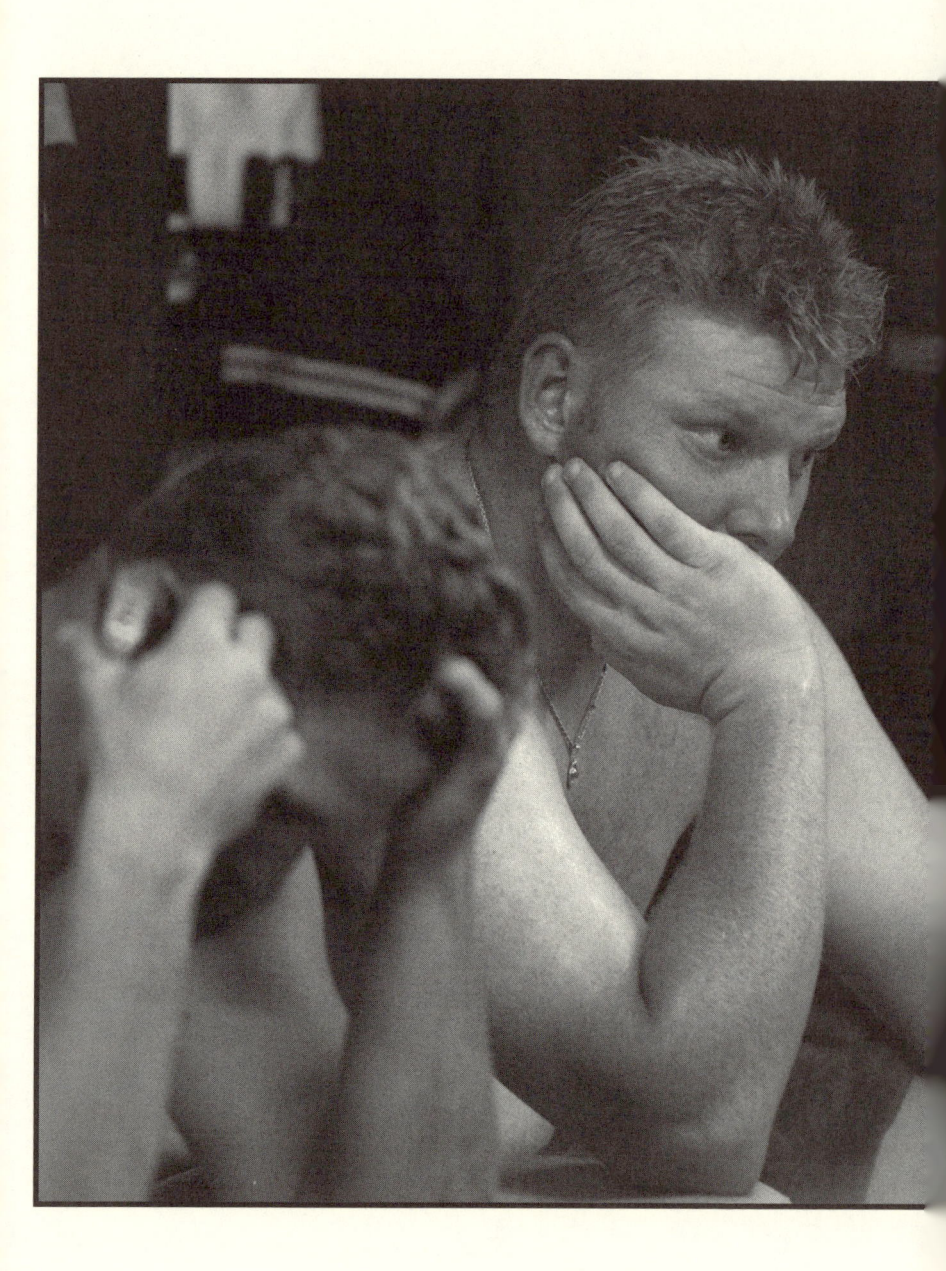

1

Outta Your Head In the Bully

ERIC COOPER leans up from his seat in the bullpen until he is directly over the fence. Then the right-handed pitcher pushes his finger against his left nostril and proceeds to honk his brains out, the overwhelming majority of the loogie going splat on the rotting wood. The rest dangles from his upper lip.

"It's like a stalactite, don't you think?" Cooper says, looking around.

Don Blaylock was sitting beside Cooper. Not any more.

"You nasty. Throw that shit on the ground, man. In a few minutes, I be slipping around on it and shit."

Brad Steele is in the bullpen. Righty. Graduate of the University of California-Berkeley. Says he had an offer to sign for $100,000 out of high school, but chose college instead. Was drafted in the late rounds and only pocketed $1,000. Has no regrets. Says baseball is great and all that, but he's a better person for going to Berkeley.

Brandon Mattingly, catcher, is in the bullpen. Played for the Otters in 2000. Feisty. Was suspended three games and fined $75 for fighting. Dips so much snuff his lower lip sticks out like

Cro-Magnon Man. Has tattoo of a burning baseball on his forearm. Sound sleeper. His fiancee painted his toenails red one morning and he didn't notice until he came to the ballpark. Lives in Evansville in the off-season and works at a Mexican restaurant. Has made up to $150 a night entertaining at bachelorette parties. Says chicks dig ballplayers.

The Otters' bully is a platform behind the right-field fence and in front of the brick wall that, generations ago, served as Bosse Field's outer limits. You get here by climbing up the side like a little kid going to the top berth of a bunk bed. Somewhat like a lifeboat, it's surprisingly roomy. Allowing for dangled legs, you could seat almost half the team.

The bullpen is maybe 300 feet from the dugout, but it may as well be that many miles. That's because there are no coaches in the bullpen.

Forget what you've seen in the majors when the TV camera zooms in on the guy warming up and there's a grownup next to him holding a clipboard and counting pitches. This is independent league ball—the lowest of the low minors—and there are barely enough coaches to fill the rectangular boxes next to first and third base, much less the ancillary locations.

The dugout is headquarters. The command center. Where the bats are kept. Where what's left of the water fountain remains. Where each sweating player wipes off with a piece of material the size of a woman's compact because the trainer could only find one towel this night and decided to cut it into pieces.

The bullpen is a remote outpost. If there is mail, it would arrive by bush pilot. Best to leave the natives in their hut like tribal militia and only call them out when the regulars have failed.

It's June, early in the season. The fireflies haven't even come out yet.

Watching baseball from the bullpen is like sitting on the neighbors' deck and looking at a game being played in your backyard.

Sometimes children work up the courage to come to our perch and ask for autographs. The boys and girls are politely told to stay on the other side of the fence so they won't be skulled by any stray home runs. But the real reason to limit access has nothing to do with head trauma. There is no toilet in the bullpen. Guys go against the brick wall or, if they're not happy with the way they're being treated on the team, into the batting cage.

How many kids dream about playing professional baseball when they get old enough?

They profess to love it more than anything they know or ever will know. Whatever it takes, they vow, doing the sign of the cross with their glove. No injury will stop them. No amount of rejection. Anything for the chance—just the chance—to be in a pay-for-play lineup.

But I wonder.

Some of these Otters are more than 1,200 miles from home. Some don't have a car. They dress in a clubhouse smaller than a bunt single. Counting time spent before the games and traveling, they earn less than minimum wage. They get $12 a day for meals. To save money, most players stay with host families, sometimes sleeping two to a bed. They are more alert to fast-food coupons than the homeless.

On some road trips, the bus leaves Bosse Field at 10:30 P.M.— or 30 minutes after the last inning—and doesn't arrive at the motel until well after daybreak.

Sometimes the bussie gets lost. Sometimes his conveyance smells like piss. Sometimes the sheets in the motel haven't been changed from the previous night's occupant. Sometimes the air-conditioning doesn't work.

If an Otter is hurt and can't play, he'll be released for a week without pay while he tries to get healthy. If the team goes out of town during this time, he'll rehab on his own in Evansville because the only trainer must stay with the club. If the young man still can't perform after seven days, he'll probably be gone for good. And he'll pay his own way home. Same deal if there's a family emergency during the 84-game season. This is the Frontier League, an outpost on the bottom rung, not a home for wayward ballplayers.

They have little life away from the field. Pre-game workouts start three hours before the game or at 4 P.M. Some come an hour or more early and help the understaffed grounds crew roll in the batting cage. Aside from Mattingly, they know next to nothing about the city. I could put a $1,000 bill in the door of the Convention and Visitors Bureau and it would go unclaimed.

On the road, they can't go anywhere even if they want to. Nobody has a car, not even the coaches. Occasionally, the motel is within walking distance of restaurants. Other times, they must rely on the pizza delivery man for both lunch and a post-game meal.

They spend afternoons before the bus leaves for the field watching "Hollywood Squares" or playing Nintendo or complaining about the coaching staff.

If a uniform gets ripped, there's no one to patch it—except the person who wears it. Some teams in the league don't have locker rooms. After the game, the players carry their equipment bags through the crowd to the bus like when they were in American Legion ball.

A team's salary cap for the season is $49,600. Minimum pay is $550 per month. No player can receive more than $1,100.

One night the umpires didn't show up and the Otters had to scramble to find two certified replacements. If nobody had stepped in, league rules stipulate that a player from each team would have been appointed emergency fill-ins at $25 per game.

The dreamers, would they still be in love with it?

"Ever played whiffle ball with a dildo?" Cooper wants to know.

Nobody has.

"It's pretty fun. Gotta learn to hit with one hand, though."

Brian Harrison jogs down the first-base line, turns left at the fence and joins the group in the bullpen.

Where he is ignored.

The first baseman, third baseman and emergency catcher tries to start a conversation with Blaylock, but his teammate turns the other way.

Harrison starts to smell his armpit as if perhaps he's to blame, but then realizes what's going on.

"You're big-leaguing me, aren't you?"

They laugh.

"Geez, you had me going," Harrison says. "I thought I had shit on my face or something."

You big-league somebody by regarding his presence as not being worthy of even a glance from your arrogant, self-centered self.

Another way to big-league a teammate is to offer advice on playing the game when your wisdom was not sought.

An inning earlier, it was the consensus of the bullpen that right fielder Mark Thomas was positioning himself way too deep. This viewpoint was shared with their teammate, whose only response was a blistering glare.

Steele says his girlfriend isn't in the stands this night.

"Good," Harrison says. "That shit you two do during the game makes me want to puke."

The infielder is referring to their habit of locking eyes and then flashing signs signaling their affection for each other in the manner of a third-base coach to a hitter.

Blaylock wonders what it means when Steele goes from his belt to his chin to his ear.

"Tongue," Mattingly guesses. "Lots of tongue."

Harrison, who is white, says he should be appointed an honorary black person. As proof, Harrison goes into something that is more a spasm than a dance. Blaylock, who is black, diplomatically says Harrison may qualify by the end of the season, but not just yet.

Cooper honks another loogie. Not wanting to use his fingers to clean up the mess, he wipes with the outfield fence.

I've never seen wood used like that.

"You get a splinter in your nose, man," Blaylock says, moving even further away.

"Doesn't that hurt your face?" Steele asks.

"You give me $100 and I'll eat it," Mattingly offers.

Cooper doesn't say anything. He is too busy watching an ant that is trapped in the mucous and swimming for its life.

"You got a condition? You taking medication or something?" Harrison asks from a safe distance.

"It's good that it's not green or yellow, don't you think?" Cooper says.

Terry Roe is in the bullpen. Lefty. Likes to drink beer. Says he is ready to come into a game after only 10 warmup tosses. Came to training camp in a 1984 Regal that has more than 280,000 miles on the odometer. Says you can't make new car payments on his Otters' salary of $600 a month. Says if he can't make it here, he'll go back to waiting tables at a country club.

Nick Stelzner is in the bullpen. Righty. Psychology major. Likes white-water rafting. Wouldn't mind being a pilot. Or an anthropologist. Went to Lewis-Clark State College in Lewiston, Idaho, where the coach believes in teaching his players to box. Everybody fights three one-minute rounds with padded gloves. Word spreads that L-C guys have to fight for their positions. Opposing teams are intimidated, Stelzner says, and the team is phenomenally successful.

B. J. Richter is in the bullpen. Right-handed submarine-style closer. Lives on farm in South Dakota. Little or no physique. Looks like an accountant. Says he enjoys reading Tony Kornheiser in

The Washington Post. Comes up to a group of teammates and says, "Hey, guys, let's have an interesting conversation." Wants to write my column for a week. Says it would be easy.

They talk about the baby rabbit that was trapped between the fence and the bullpen gate the previous night, Stelzner's lucky number (624), the groupies outside the locker room at Billings, Mont., one of Blaylock's former coaches who only has one leg, Roe's gut, and how Cooper didn't get along with his coach at Texas Tech because the guy thought he was a pussy for having asthma attacks.

Blaylock holds the walkie-talkie that is the line of communication to the dugout. It rarely works. Too much static. Wrong channel. Dead batteries. Pick your poison.

The procedure is supposed to go like this: When manager Dan Shwam gets tired of watching his starting pitcher being hammered, he tells pitching coach Britt Carmichael to get so-and-so reliever loosened up.

Carmichael asks how quick.

The skip will either grunt, which means take the normal amount of time, or he will roll his arms in the manner of a basketball referee indicating a walking violation, which means as fast as goddamn possible.

The pitching coach then stands on the top dugout step and raises his hand like back in school when he knew the correct answer.

This tells Blaylock to turn the unit on, which he does.

Carmichael: "RZZT, SCRTT, FRZZ."

Blaylock, dutifully: "Bullpen to dugout. Bullpen to dugout. Sheep to shepherd. Sheep to shepherd. Over."

Carmichael, louder: "PZZT, THZZ, Steele, GRZZ, SCHRZZ."

Blaylock, to Steele: "You're going in."

Steele: "When?"

Blaylock, shaking the device in an effort to improve reception: "Don't know."

Carmichael, becoming more agitated: "FZZT, FZZT, FZZT."

Blaylock: "Did not copy that. Repeat. Did not copy. When is Steele going in? Now or the next inning? Over."

Carmichael, frantically: "CRZZ. CRZZ. CRZZ."

Stelzner: "Britt should have a separate signal for each pitcher. Wouldn't have to go through all this. Hand on head is Steele. Hand on elbow is Blaylock. Hand on balls is Roe."

Carmichael: "TCCKT. TCCKT. TCCKT."

Blaylock, earnestly: "Now or next inning? Now or next inning? Over. Move your mouth away from the receiver. Maybe that will help."

Carmichael: "URGTT. URGTT. URGTT."

Stelzner: "I've heard of radio silence, but this is ridiculous."

Cooper: "Where is Marconi when you need him?"

Blaylock, excitedly: "The static is lifting. The static is lifting. I'm starting to understand him."

Carmichael, clear as a bell: "Aw, fuck."

Steele isn't happy in the bullpen. Normally a starter, he says he can't get accustomed to getting warmed two or more times a night and maybe or maybe not getting in the game.

He's also a worrywart.

"Am I ready?" Steele asks after five minutes of popping Mattingly's glove.

"Only you know that, dude," Cooper replies.

"I don't think I'm ready."

He throws some more.

Cooper says the bullpen should hook a strong rope to the right-field fence and pull it back if an opposing hitter launches a bomb to that area.

Blaylock shakes his head.

"The rope would break and we would all fall down and shit."

An Otter lines out to shortstop. He runs the remaining 80 feet and touches first base.

I ask why.

"It's a fine if you don't," Stelzner explains. "We're poor enough already."

Steele does more stomach crunches.

"I'm not loose," he says.

"You're fucking loose," Mattingly says. "Get outta your head."

"I don't know whether I want to pitch or not," Steele says agonizingly. "I just don't know."

"Shit, dude, you complain when you do and you complain when you don't," Cooper says.

Carmichael has put the walkie-talkie aside. He takes a step on the field, points to Steele and waves his cap.

"I think I feel OK," Steele says. "My slider is dirty out here, but I don't know about out there."

He grabs his jacket and turns to me.

"Write the first five chapters of your book about how bad I am."

We watch him walk to the mound.

"Hitters can feel if a pitcher doesn't have any confidence," Harrison says. "It's like a sixth sense. You watch. Whatever he throws, they're gonna jack."

Steele promptly gives up two hits and Springfield closes the gap to 3-2.

Stelzner is brought in to close out the ninth. He can't. They tie the game with two out.

Even as far away as we are, it's clear that Stelzner is flamed as he walks off the field.

"Oh, God," Cooper says. "I mean, oh, God."

"What's the matter?" Blaylock asks. "You get some of that nasty shit in your eyes or something?"

"Nick's my roommate. When he gets lit up, he's horrible to be with. He sits around all night all pissed off. I don't even want to go home."

An Otter is picked off first base. The bullpen hollers that the umpire beats his wife.

The goal of every player at this level is to be picked up by a major league team's farm system. In their parlance, to make it to affiliated ball.

It does happen. At the beginning of the 2001 season, 41 Frontier League alums—including two Otters—were on current minor-league rosters from Triple-A down to rookie ball.

Morgan Burkhart and Brian Tollberg are the biggest success stories.

Burkhart, a first baseman, went undrafted out of high school and college and found a construction job, thinking his baseball career was over. But he caught on with the Richmond, Ind., Roosters and played four years until the Boston Red Sox signed him to a minor league contract in 1998. He made it to the big club for 25 games the following year and spent much of 2000 and 2001 at Pawtucket, their Triple-A affiliate.

Tollberg, formerly of the Chillicothe, Ohio, Paints, won 10 games for the San Diego Padres during the 2001 season.

Realistically, the only call these Otters can expect is from their parents asking when they're going to quit this nonsense and come home.

They're at this level for a reason. The position players are too small, or they don't have enough power, or they aren't considered durable enough to play more than short-season ball. The pitchers can't throw 90 miles per hour, or they don't have much of a breaking ball, or they lose their composure when teammates boot balls in the field.

Or they don't have enough experience.

Blaylock, of Fort Worth, Texas, hadn't pitched in a game since junior college in 1999. He couldn't get his credits to transfer, so he got a job as an auto mechanic. His claim to fame is working on former Texas Ranger Oddibe McDowell's car.

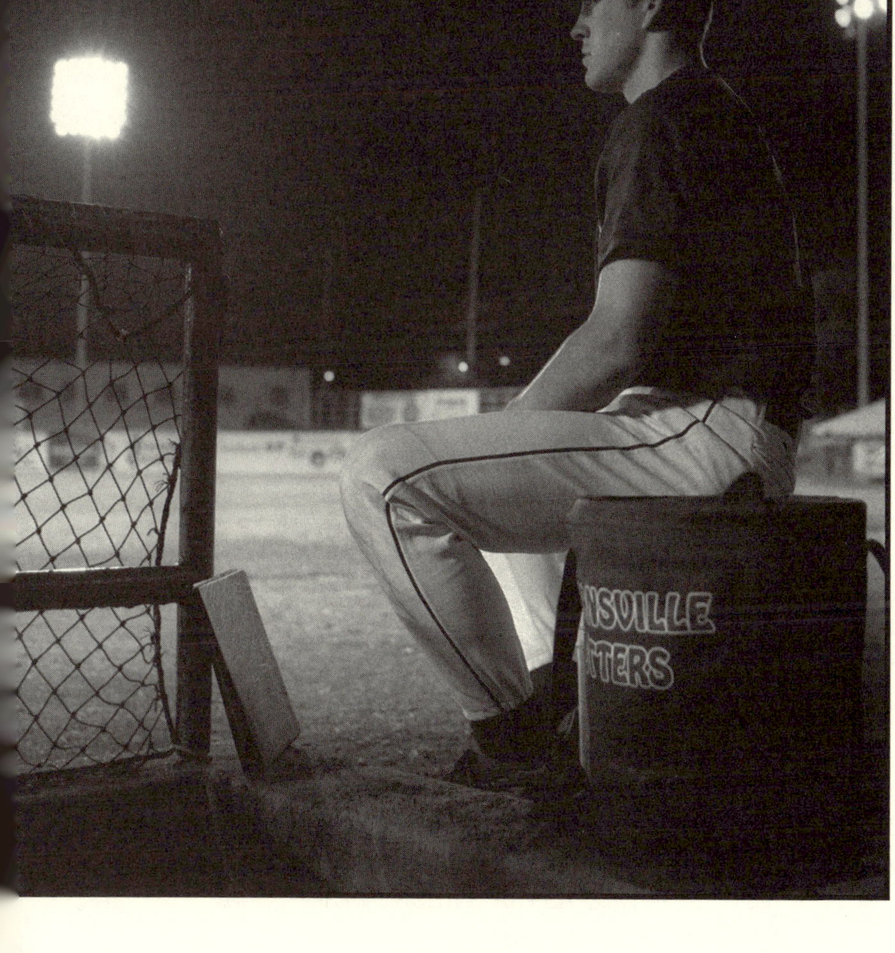

But broach the subject of getting signed out of this league and there's more hope than at a Billy Graham rally.

These players believe scouts attend every Frontier League game by the van load. They don't announce their presence because they don't want to spook the players. But they're somewhere. Down the first-base line. Behind home plate. In the hot dog line. Have a good game and, poof, like magic, one will appear outside the team bus with a big cigar, a "Hiya, kid" and a contract.

They believe their former coaches are working 12 hours a day making calls to teams on their behalf. Never mind spending time with their wives and kids. Never mind watching reality TV. They have phones attached to their ears saying, "Boy, have I got a third baseman for you" or "I know a left-handed reliever you can get for a song and a Power Bar."

These Otters believe they're so close to making it. Fine-tune that overhand delivery or make that swing a little more level and the ticket out of Evansville will come.

Who cares that the Mets, Astros, Mariners, Marlins, Yankees, Cubs, Braves, Tigers, Reds, Phillies, Pirates, Giants, Brewers and Orioles aren't interested? Maybe the Devil Rays are. They just have a hard time showing it.

Frontier League rules mandate that teams may keep no more than seven players with one year in the pros, two with two years and three so-called veterans with unlimited professional experience, but no one older than 27. The rest must be newbies.

Those who have played at the pro level have been released at least once and often several times. Even the rookies are rejects because they weren't selected in the professional draft.

The independent league is almost certainly their last chance. If they can't put up dominating numbers here, where can they put up dominating numbers?

So there's one thing worse than the low pay, the long bus

rides, pre-game meals of peanut-butter sandwiches and dugouts that have bubble gum stuck to the walls like so many Post-It Notes.

Getting released.

More precisely, worrying about getting released.

God, my batting average has dropped to under .250 and I haven't played in three days. Am I gone?

Shit, I missed a bunt sign and the coach hasn't said a word to me for a week. Am I gone?

Many of the players are college graduates or just a few credits short, so they likely have something in the private sector to fall back on.

But most majored in baseball.

When two or more are gathered together, they talk about how good Jim Edmonds of the St. Louis Cardinals is at going back on fly balls and how nobody has ever thrown a better curve ball than Pedro Martinez. Pitchers grab oranges and throw imaginary sinkers. Hitters pick up fingernail files and take imaginary cuts at the plate.

They religiously watch "Baseball Tonight" on ESPN. A game highlight isn't just a highlight. It's the inspiration for a story of a brush with greatness.

Sportscaster: "The Cubs continue to maintain their lead in the NL Central, taking care of the Dodgers, 4-3."

Otter: "I played with a guy in Bakersfield who lockered across from Kerry Wood in spring training. He said the dude's goatee looks like crap, but he's got legs bigger than tree trunks."

Other Otter: "My buddy was at the Dodger camp in Vero Beach. He's standing there adjusting his cup and Sandy Koufax comes by in a golf cart. Wasn't looking where he was going and almost ran over his toe."

Another Otter: "I would've put my foot there on purpose. People would ask why I was limping and I'd say, 'Sandy Koufax, man.'"

Sportscaster: "In other National League action, the San Francisco Giants ran off and left the Expos, winning 12-0. Andres Galarraga led the way with three hits and four RBI."

Otter: "I pitched against Galarraga in an exhibition game in college."

Other Otter: "How'd you do?"

Otter: "Got him out the first time. Thought I was some kind of hot shit. I smoothed the dirt around the mound like it was no big deal, but inside I was busting up."

Other Otter: "What happened his next time up?"

Otter: "Hit a bomb 500 feet."

Growing up, they were always the stars of their teams. The first kid chosen at the Mustang League player draft. The shortstop when he wasn't pitching. The cleanup hitter. The player adults from other leagues tried to steal.

As teens, they were selected to traveling teams that crisscrossed the country. In college, they played in prestigious summer leagues from Cap Cod to Alaska.

As Otters, they can wear a different all-star T-shirt under their uniform each day for a month and not have to do laundry.

Playing baseball is The Known. Not playing is territory they don't want to chart—territory they are afraid to chart.

So they sit in a bullpen hundreds of miles from home and watch the ant finally die in Cooper's mucous.

"Health department violation and shit," Blaylock says.

The game goes into extra innings. Stelzner settles down and pitches a scoreless tenth.

Richter keeps a notebook on opposing hitters. He watches to see who overstrides, who leans out over the plate, who can't hit a pitch over the outside corner, who chases sinkers. Then he meticulously writes down each factoid.

Baseball does not permit a pitcher to bring his crib sheet to the mound. Something about keeping the time of a game under six hours.

I look through his entries. Can you remember all this?

"Certainly. I attribute several outs every season to the documentation on these pages."

Attribution. Documentation. He does read Kornheiser.

Sometimes Richter talks about playing just because he loves to compete. He'll say he realizes the Frontier League is as far as he's going to get in professional baseball. He'll say he is just playing for the thrill of getting guys out and being on a team.

Then he'll register a couple of clutch saves and talk about playing winter ball. A lot of guys get seen in those leagues, he says, eyes flashing. Maybe Evansville isn't the end. Maybe I can move up.

"What I really want is to pitch the perfect inning," he says. "Know the tendencies of each hitter. Put every ball where they can't hit it. Walking off the mound would be the greatest feeling in the world. That hasn't happened yet so I still have my motivation."

Carmichael wants Roe for the 11th inning. Forget waving hats. Forget the radio. Forget smoke signals. He cups his mouth with his hands and slowly spells out "R-O-E."

Blaylock is disappointed. He has been up three different times and thrown the equivalent of half a game.

"You got dry-humped, dude," Cooper says by way of consolation.

The Otters go quietly in the 10th and Roe enters the game.

Blaylock climbs back up to the bullpen. Head in hand, he stares out at the pitcher's mound.

"C'mon, Terry," he hollers. "Have a good inning. Hum babe."

Then he clams up. One round of encouragement is enough.

I wonder how Blaylock can root for Roe even that much.

It's probably not possible to get out of the Frontier League if you strike out every other man you face and only allow earned runs on Bastille Day.

It is definitely impossible to vacate these premises if you don't get in the game.

In Little League, the players were "Yea, team" because after every third victory, the coach would take them all to the Dairy Queen in the back of his pickup truck for milkshakes. In high school and college, they wanted to do well as a unit so their drill sergeant of a coach wouldn't make them run wind sprints up the hill beside the septic tank.

In independent league ball, it's all about being more selfish than a couple of six-year-old boys in a sandbox.

Winning makes for more towel-slapping in the clubhouse, but the simple truth is exit visas are based on numbers—a player's numbers, not the team's.

For instance, a guy starts every game at second base for the team that wins the championship. Solid .285 hitter. Almost never makes an error. Leads the team in sacrifice bunts. Leads the team in sacrifice flies. Leads the team in moving runners from second to third with less than two out. Leads the team in turning double plays and the award that goes with it—17 spike wounds to the shins.

He earns a hammy handshake from his manager for a job well done—particularly the night he went down on a close force play like he had been run over by a lawn tractor, but held onto the ball.

But there is no telephone call.

A more likely candidate for a contract from a big league organization would be the first sacker on a team that finished 20 games back and whose whole season was one extended funeral. He fielded like a mine sweeper run aground, doesn't know anybody's first name and doesn't care, never once gave himself up for the good of the squad and was voted most likely to take up space by his teammates.

But he had 15 bombs and a slugging percentage to die for. Bye-bye. See you later.

Roe throws two effective innings and the Otters win on a home run in the bottom of the 12th.

"Good job, Roe," Blaylock says just loud enough to be heard as he walks to the dugout.

Cooper hollers from deep right field.

"The rabbit, dude. He's gone."

At least somebody has gotten out of here.

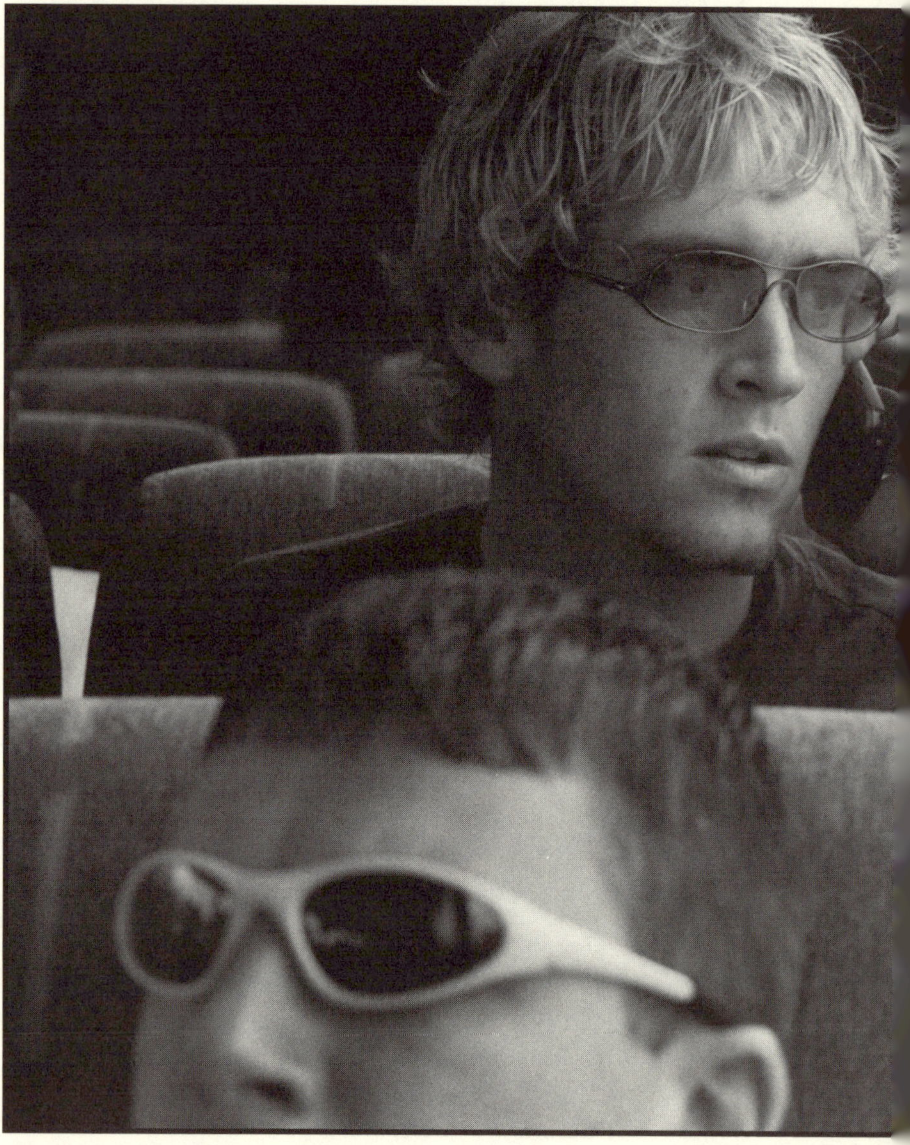

2

The Last Cut is the Deepest

MAY 19

"The scouts have said no to every man in this room. They think you're not good enough. Prove they're wrong."

The Otters are getting their first look at manager Dan Shwam. Fortysomething. Glasses. White-haired. Paunch. Ill-fitting jeans. Bad knee. Runs worse than Lasorda.

"Don't give me a non-baseball reason to release you. Play ball and go back to your host family and get your rest. Don't buy a bottle of Jack and start waving it on Main Street."

A player says he drove to Evansville from California and doesn't have enough money left for a Hershey Bar.

"Don't be waving that either," Shwam advises.

He tells them nothing is better than playing baseball and getting paid for it.

"You're not punching a clock somewhere like your buddies. I coached a guy once in the Northern League who wrote '9 to 5' on his cap. Whenever he thought the game was horseshit, he'd take his hat off and realize what he'd be doing otherwise. Cheered him up every damn time."

Speaking of hats, Shwam says there aren't enough right now for a team picture.

The players who were among the previous year's Otters wince. They've been down this road before.

Charles Jacey was in his last season as owner. Bills weren't getting paid. Equipment wasn't being ordered. Opening Day rolled around. No caps. Then-manager Greg Tagert had to go to a sporting goods store. Some of the hats were too small and guys wore them like beanies. Some were too big and looked like maroon frying pans.

Apparently, Shwam has heard the story.

"But you *will* have headwear. And it *will* fit."

More announcements.

Payday is the first and 15th of the month. Don't spend it all in one place. Suggestion: Learn to like tuna.

The Booster Club will provide three meals a day during training camp.

Be respectful of your host family, Shwam tells them. Even if you've eaten like a hummingbird all day, don't empty their refrigerator at 3 o'clock in the morning.

It's OK for the batboys to run errands and bring you something to eat. But for Christ's sake, tip them a dollar or two. Don't be cheap bastards.

You have free memberships at Tri-State Athletic Club. Use the weight room. The season will beat you down. Lift to build yourselves back up.

"Don't call me 'Coach,' or 'Mister,' or 'Sir.' Shit, I feel old enough at it is. 'Skip' is fine. 'Shwamie' is fine. Anything my wife would call me is fine.

"Don't bring those damn cellphones on the practice field. The last thing we need is for a guy to be hitting, get distracted by ringing from somebody's equipment bag and be whacked up side the head.

"Pitching is No. 1 in my book. We pitch. We defend. We win. The next week will be very competitive. First guy with a sore arm goes home.

"I don't want your lifetime goal to be an Otter. Don't get comfortable here. I want you to be a Cub, a Cardinal, a Marlin. I run tryout camps. I have connections. I can get you moved up."

Jacey, a New Jersey businessman, owned the franchise from 1996 until April of 2001. The Bussing family, longtime fixtures in Evansville, purchased a 52 percent share. Bill is an attorney. His father, Bud, is a real estate developer. Bill's wife, Phyllis, is director of schools for the Catholic Diocese of Evansville. His sister, Dr. Marie Bussing-Burks, is a professor at the University of Southern Indiana. His brother-in-law, Barry Burks, owns several stores in the Evansville area.

The Goldklang Group owns the remaining 48 percent and will be in charge of the team on the field. It operates professional baseball franchises in Charleston, S. C., Fort Myers, Fla., Hudson Valley, N.Y., St. Paul, Minn., and Sioux Falls, S. D.

Marv Goldklang, a former Wall Street lawyer, heads the Group. Mike Veeck, the son of the late Hall of Fame owner and master promoter Bill Veeck, is president of three of the teams and has worked with all five.

Mark Shuster, an executive vice president, will oversee the new Evansville entry. His wife, the former Patricia Edwards, is an Evansville native and her family has known the Bussings for decades. She's the one who suggested to Mark that Bill, Bud et al might be good business partners.

Tom Whaley, who worked in corporate sales for the Tampa Bay Devil Rays, is chief executive officer for Goldklang. Van Schley, a longtime baseball man, helps the team find players.

Actor Bill Murray—who appeared in the movies "Ghostbusters," "Caddyshack" and "What About Bob?"—is also a member of the investment group. He visits his properties as often as his film schedule permits. The talk is that he'll visit Bosse Field at least once.

Jacey fired Tagert, who had taken the team to the playoffs in each of his four seasons. Although Shwam was Jacey's hire, he was no stranger to the members of the Goldklang Group who knew him from his many years in the Northern League. Tagert landed the job as field boss of the rival Dubois County Dragons, an hour away in Huntingburg, Ind.

Jim Miller, the only general manager the team has had, was retained by the new owners. He and wife Pam are known around Evansville as being as married to the Otters as they are to each other.

Tagert was well-liked in Evansville by the fans and players. Lanky. Bookish. Mid-30s. Direct descendant of Ichabod Crane.

The worst thing the players from the 2000 Otters had to say about him was they sure did a lot of running in training camp. Tagert is an avid jogger, sometimes putting in eight miles a day. Guys had to run a mile in 5:45 to make the team. Every day after on-field workouts, the streets around Bosse Field looked like the proving grounds for marathoners. Wheezing young men in baseball shirts leaned against lampposts. Any home run trot was going to be easy.

Tagert supervised the pre-game stretching and used the opportunity to joke with a pitcher who was dating one of the beer girls, and to ask his backup catcher, a surfer, if he's found a wave shop in Southern Indiana.

He is affable, encouraging, approachable.

"Tags is like a diplomat," one player said. "Every day it's like he's got 24 stops to make. Each guy on the team gets a chunk of his time."

"You can be the last man on the bench and know you're going to play at least a couple of times a week," another said. "You might pinch-hit. You might pinch-run. Nobody gets down on himself. Everybody stays in the game."

Tagert rarely lectured his players. Almost never got mad.

"We like him," another player said. "You play better for somebody you like."

Dan Shwam puts his leg up on the bench in front of him. Or tries to. The limb stays there for a couple of seconds and falls back.

"Gimp," he mutters.

A golden opportunity for a budding team comedian to crack wise.

Nothing.

Is this a guy who likes to have his chops busted by people half his age? How familiar do they dare get with him?

One thing is for sure. The vibe isn't right now.

Might be later.

Might not.

"Training camp starts at 9 A.M. tomorrow," Shwam says, "and it will last until we get all our work done. I know Evansville is a Las Vegas-type town and all that."

Chuckles.

"But don't be making any plans until after 5."

A player says he works for a company that sells nutritional supplements and can get free samples.

"This is the Frontier League," Shwam replies. "Free is good."

MAY 20

Counting non-roster invitees, there are about 50 guys doing what baseball players have done since Abner Doubleday posted the first practice schedule.

Trying to impress the coach.

One young man is wearing sweatpants, sweatshirt and a thick pullover on this hot morning to prove he is in such good condition he doesn't need to dress sanely.

Another is running in place beside third base. He holds his arm out as if setting the bar and goes harder and harder and higher and higher until his knees touch the target. One minute passes. Then two. Sod flies around his feet. This guy is a machine. Give him a season and he could excavate a stadium.

Another would-be Otter is hitting himself fly balls. He sends the ball straight up in the air, grabs his glove and settles under the self-induced pop-up.

Then there's Spectacular Catch. You played it as a kid. Now watch it performed by a group of 24-year-olds.

Same deal as tryouts for the Babe Ruth League all-stars. A pitcher, who is trying to show off his wares, pitches. A hitter, who is trying to show that line drives are his business, hits. Most everyone else shags balls.

They stand in the outfield an interminable amount of time waiting for a ball to come their way. Finally, Santa sends one of them a scorcher. It has the perfect trajectory for what he has in mind. It's a win-win. If he misses the ball, no runs will score, no game will be lost and no coach will be flamed. But if he snares it... If he extends himself in the manner of an Acapulco cliff diver, perhaps ball will find leather an inch off the ground. Maybe a bunch of teammates will whoop and holler. Maybe the skipper will say, shit, this guy can really run down the baseball.

The secret is not reacting right away. That would mean catching the ball in stride. Can't have that. There's a team to make. Lingering a fraction of a second means a collision course with the outfield grass and an opportunity to prove that his nose can withstand a crash landing while he continues to clutch the object of everyone's attention.

Watching from the back of the batting cage are the assistant coaches.

Todd Brown, 25, played for the Otters the previous two seasons. Nickname is "Sweetpea." Has played every position except catcher, pitcher and center field. Wants to be a high school coach. Will work with hitters. Could be activated if there's an injury or a starter isn't producing.

Ron Ryan, 38, will also coach the hitters during training camp and at home games. Elementary school principal and assistant baseball coach at Brescia (Ky.) College. Nicknamed "Sasquatch" because of back hair. First year in pro ball. Won't go on most road trips.

Britt Carmichael, 25, is the pitching coach. Younger than some of the players. Portly. Leads league in saying "flustrated." Pitching coach at Lubbock (Tex.) Christian University. Has never worked at the professional level.

And Shwam.

The 42-year-old is a math teacher at Highland High School in Salt Lake City, Utah, where he is head coach of the baseball team and an assistant to the basketball coach. This is his 11th summer in the independent leagues. He prefers this to affiliated ball because he wants to make out his own lineup and not be told who must play by somebody 500 miles away wearing an expensive polo shirt with the team's logo on the front.

When Greg Tagert looks at you, he's usually grinning. It's as if he's waiting for you to make a joke about how he jogs like a penguin, so you can have a good laugh.

This guy Shwam just looks at you.

"I'm going to treat these men like professionals," Shwam explains. "It's not like college where you hover over them all the time. This is their job. If they need me to prop them up, they're in the wrong line of work. I'll manage like this is Double-A or Triple-A. The coaches communicate. I'm the hammer. The bad guy. I'm not going to be a rah-rah person. When I'm at school, I like it when I go three-four weeks and don't hear from my principal. That means I'm doing what I'm supposed to be doing. That's the attitude I want these guys to have."

Auditions are over for the day. Shwam motions for everyone to gather around home plate.

He says he likes what he sees and believes there's enough talent for an "A" team and a "B" team.

"But the league has already made out the schedule for just

the one team from Evansville, so that's what we'll have to go with."

Hmm. Shwam's "A" team gets a daily food allowance equal to a chopped steak, baked potato and small salad. All the money is gone. The other contingent would have to subsist on dumpster leavings.

He tells them he isn't going to micro-manage games.

"Our catchers will call the game. Don't be looking in the dugout for a bunch of finger-to-the-ear, finger-to-the-nose shit. It's your career, not mine. Same way on the bases. We're going to run. Some of you will earn the right to steal whenever you think you've got the pitcher figured out. If you get thrown out, I'm not going to cut off your balls. Getting signed out of this league is the name of the game. That means making plays. You making the plays. Not me."

The pocket schedules are in for the season that begins May 30 and ends Aug. 28. There are 12 games each with five Western Division foes—Dubois County, River City (in O'Fallon, Mo., a St. Louis suburb), Springfield, Ill., Gateway (in Collinsville, Ill., on the East side of St. Louis) and Cook County (in Crestwood, Ill., one of the South Chicago suburbs). There are four games (two home and two away) with the six Eastern Division clubs—Canton, Ill.; Chillicothe, Ohio; Richmond, Ind.; Johnstown, Pa.; Kalamazoo, Mich., and London in Ontario, Canada.

"This is the first time in all the years I've played that one of these things has been in color," one impressed would-be Otter says as he grabs a handful.

Other players who have been through the long haul of a professional season look over the schedule to count the number of off days. There are three built in to the all-star break in July and seven altogether. One is the day after the 325-mile return trip from Chillicothe. One is the day of the 270-mile bus ride to Cook County. One is the day of the 600-mile trek to London.

"Looking for a title to your book?" one young man asks.
Certainly.
"Call it, 'From Here to Eternity.'"
Overheard on the way out of the ballpark:
"You got a car?"
"No."
"Know anybody who does? It's a five-mile walk back to the motel, dude."
"Ask that kid over there in the Rangers' cap. Somebody said they heard him ask where to buy gas."
"Then it must be real, man."
"Why?"
"Ain't gonna be filling up his lawn mower out here."

MAY 22

Mark Shuster estimates the Otters need to draw 3,000 a night for the team to break even.

"Evansville has, what, around 130,000 people and that goes up to almost 200,000 when you take in the metropolitan area. The fan base is certainly here.

"But we're realistic. We know we're not going to turn a profit this year. These things take time. You have to have a plan and you have to work at it. Charlie Jacey is a nice guy, but he was trying to run the operation from New Jersey. That's impossible."

Shuster says part of the agreement with Jacey was that the vendor debt of around $50,000 would be tacked on to the purchase price.

"We heard the stories about how they tried to get the beer guy to take an outfield billboard instead of a check. That kind of thing wasn't well-received and it probably caused some bad feelings. But all that's in the past. Everybody has been paid and we're moving ahead.

"We're going to triple the marketing budget. The sales staff will be nine instead of two. It's all about promotions and giving people a sense of unpredictability. We're going to have fireworks. We're going to have drink specials. We're going to have giveaways. Fans want to forget about their lives for three hours. They're putting us in charge of their fun. That's a good job to have."

MAY 23

Lisa Rust used to live two blocks from Bosse Field and always wanted to host a player, but considered her house too old and too small. Then she bought a larger place and decided to be a host mom.

"I told the front office I have a 13-year-old son and two Labrador retrievers," she says. "I told them my player needs his own vehicle because I can't be stopping what I'm doing to take him to the field. I also said he can't be afraid of large dogs. My boy will be spending much of the summer at camp, so my summer son could have his room.

"I arrived at the field at the appointed time to pick up my Otter. The players were still practicing. It was interesting to look them over and try to guess which one I would be bringing home. It felt like I was picking up a new puppy.

"There was some confusion. I found out that Scott Suraci would be my player, but he had been told I hadn't shown up so he went back to the motel.

"We finally made connections. Scott is very nice and as shy as he is tall. He said he had a buddy on the team and wondered if I could take him in. Scott said the friend has a vehicle, but he doesn't. I thought, hmm, so much for the team honoring my request about transportation.

"That was all right with me, so Jeremy Coronado entered my life. Turns out, there was room to move the full-size bed over and put a mattress on the floor.

"Then the next day, both summer sons asked if there was any way I could handle one more Otter. I asked aloud why three guys would want to shove themselves in one not-very-big space. They said when you play baseball, you get used to sleeping as many as five to a room. I said, well, if it doesn't bother you, it won't bother me. That's how Chris Cosbey became part of the household.

"They went to Wal-Mart and brought back stackable crates for shoes and such. They hang their clothes from the rafters and burn candles to get rid of the smell of the dogs and my cigarette smoke.

"I moved our stuff out of the kitchen pantry so each guy could have a shelf. It's full of pasta, peanut butter and all these containers of special powders for athletes.

"Jeremy is afraid of dogs. He really starts scrambling when my biggest Lab head-butts the door open and runs in. He spends most of his time reading his Bible and watching religious tapes. Scott is good about leaving notes about when they're leaving and when they're coming back. Chris hardly talks at all. Smiles a lot, though, so I guess he's happy.

"They get up at 11 o'clock to work out at the fitness place. Then it's straight to the ballpark. I'm getting the feeling I won't see them too much except on off days."

MAY 24

Five Otters from the 2000 team are still in camp. Andy Miller, son of the general manager, is one of them.

He was a utility player for Tagert. A good fielder and a .250 hitter. Usually was the smallest guy on the field.

If young Miller can't make it with Shwam, he has fallback employment without having to leave the field.

Grounds crew.

Or as he likes to call it: Dirtbagger.

Been doing it for years. Lining the basepaths. Raking the mound. Hosing down the dust. Seeing how fast he can drive the little tractor around the infield.

The kid is filthy 10 minutes into his day.

Hence the name.

Andy Miller tells me dirtbagging commands a fee of $6 an hour.

"If I make the team, we're talking $650 or something like that a month. Working on the field, with all the hours I put in, is almost double that."

Let me get this straight. The fellow who takes up the bases after the game earns considerably more than the guys who touch the bases during the game.

"That's right. Not even close."

Andy Miller believes he has an 85 percent chance of making the team. And not as a fill-in.

"I've worked hard in the off-season to be an everyday player. Last year, I was terrible at the plate. I can jump it 50 points. Easy."

So how is camp going?

"Every intrasquad game I've gotten at least one hit. I'm catching everything that's hit to me and throwing guys out on the bases.

"Plus the fact that I didn't get enough at-bats last year to be (counted as) a veteran. Why wouldn't Shwam want to keep a second-year player who only counts on his roster as a rookie? Besides that, I'm a familiar face. Fans like familiar faces."

I asked how bad it would hurt if he got cut.

"I would be very disappointed. I want to wear the uniform. I'd spend the rest of the afternoon wondering what I did wrong."

And the next day?

"I'd be back on the tractor,"

Rebecca Canterbury, 22, is the trainer. Home stands, road trips—she is the sole medical provider for 84 games. The young woman is freshly graduated from the University of Northern Iowa with a degree in looking after dinged-up athletes. This is her first job.

More than a little shy, she is having trouble adjusting to a dugout full of guys.

"I mean, they're gross. Yesterday one of them spit on the concrete floor. It was so big that bubbles came up. I'm thinking, get away from it. Just leave it there. But he came over and stirred it real carefully with the top of his shoe. It was like he wanted to preserve it or something. I don't know if I can stand it or not. I'm starting to think maybe I've made the wrong career choice."

Then there's the cussing, the snotting, the scratching and dipping so much snuff it overflows its banks and dribbles down their chins.

"The thing that gets me is that they're always talking about 'my girlfriend this' and 'my girlfriend that.' It s unbelievable. There's actually some female back home who can stand to be within 10 feet of them. How, I have no idea."

Becka, as she is called, inherited a medical cabinet that contained 18 boxes of gauze and little else.

"Nobody said anything about budget so I ordered $1,200 worth of tape, pre-wraps, ice bags, Band-Aids and ibuprofen. The cabinet isn't bare any more. I hope I don't get in trouble."

The trainer's room, such as it is, is beside the showers. Naturally, there isn't a door.

"The first few times I knocked on the locker room door and said I wasn't coming in until everybody had his pants on. I'm thinking, OK, they want me to treat their arms and their quads, so they'll get at least a little bit more dressed."

Let me guess. They got a little bit more undressed.

"I'm waiting out in the hall and nothing is happening. I started to realize, hey, my work is past that door. If I don't go in, I'll be late for work. I sneaked in with head bent over and eyes straight down. I wanted them to know there was absolutely nothing in that locker room that I wanted to see.

"The guys keep telling me it's no big deal and just to walk in like I'm part of the team. I'm trying to do that, but it isn't easy. If there was a male trainer plus me, I wouldn't feel so self-conscious. But it's just me and...them."

If she found an Otter who spits only two or three times an hour, could she, well, you know?

"Go out with him? I don't think it would be possible. Some force inside me would pop up and say 'Are you crazy?'"

MAY 25

It is a few minutes after practice at Bosse Field and a player brushes past me mumbling obscenities. He gives the ticket booth a forearm shiver, kicks the nacho stand and shares F-bombs with the children playing in the fountain across the street.

Shwam explains.

"Had to cut him. Wasn't hitting worth a damn. He might later on, but I need somebody now."

So, the guy lit into you pretty good?

"Oh, yeah, I expect it. You have to let them vent. I just sit there and take it. They say the city is shitty and the organization is shitty and I'm shitty. I just nod my head.

"The easy way would be to put the list of cuts on the board and go about my business. I know some teams that make the trainer do it.

"But I'm not like that. Nobody leaves this team without knowing why he was released. Maybe I didn't have a position for him. Maybe he had one bad day at camp and the guy he was competing with had no bad days. He might not want to hear it, but I'm going to tell him anyway."

In the locker room, pitcher Nick Stelzner, a player from last year's team, says he was almost late for training camp.

"It's 1,300 miles from Boise, Idaho, to Evansville. I'm fine for a few hours and then the radiator starts smoking. Mechanic tells me the hose clamp is bad. He replaces it and I'm on my way. Halfway across Nebraska, two tires go flat. I go into my billfold again. A few more hours of clear sailing and the radiator is smoking again. I pull into the nearest dealership. This guy tells me the hose clamp wasn't put on right, but he doesn't have time to fix it.

"I told him, 'Dude, I've got to get to Indiana to play ball.' He just looked at me. I said, 'screw this,' so I got some tools and did the job myself. I got here, so I guess I did OK."

Stelzner was the Otters' closer for the 2000 season. He only gave up three earned runs after mid-June when he joined the team following Lewis & Clark's appearance in the NAIA World Series.

He gave serious thought to retiring last September when he wasn't picked up by an affiliated team.

"What do I have to do to impress somebody? Give up two runs a season? Or none? I'm almost 90 (mph) on the radar gun. I drive more than halfway across the country to play. What do they want from me?

"I went the whole winter telling myself I was done. I want to see new things, meet new people, make enough money to afford to go to a decent restaurant. Then I did some throwing. Nice and easy. Relaxed. I was popping the glove pretty good. Some people I trust said my stuff was still nasty. I got more serious with my workouts. I asked myself if I wanted to come back to Evansville and play for almost nothing and not see my family for more than three months. I answered, hell, yes. Nothing grabs hold of you like baseball."

Another familiar face from the 2000 season is pitcher Cliff Brand, who came to the team after being released by Duluth in the Northern League. He posted a 7-3 mark for the Otters as a starter.

"Shwam is a no-nonsense guy," Brand says. "No jokes. No small talk. You don't say much to him because you don't know how he'll take it. Tagert was always messing around with you. During a critical time in the game, he'd turn around from the top of the dugout and say, 'You forgot your belt.' It never failed. You could swear up and down that you put it on, but you'd look down for just an instant and he'd say 'Gotcha.' I don't know if it helped us win or not, but we probably had the loosest dugout in the league."

Brandon Mattingly did the bulk of the catching on the 2000 team after midseason when the regular guy got hurt. Stocky but small, he lost 15 pounds to finish the year at 175 pounds.

"Last year, Tags brought nine catchers to camp," he says. "Only three this time around, so we're doing a lot more throwing."

He's fine with that. It's the muscles around his ribs that are hurting.

"Took too many practice swings the first day. I'm just now getting back to normal. I've probably fallen a little behind."

He doesn't hesitate when asked if he is going to be the opening day catcher.

"Damn right."

Shwam is high on Jewell Williams, a 6-3, 220-pound outfielder who was picked by Cleveland in the 11th round of the 1995 draft and has bounced around the minors from Akron to the New York-Pennsylvania League. Nobody in camp has anything like Williams' physique. Looks like Sonny Liston. Bull neck. Powerful forearms. A chest that could stop small-arms fire.

"This guy is the closest we have to a pedigree player," Shwam says. "We get 12-15 jacks out of his bat and we'll be rolling."

How good is Williams?

"He's taken two lockers," Stelzner says, "and nobody has said a word."

MAY 26

The players assemble like this is homeroom and it's time for morning announcements.

Shwam says the demand for host families exceeds supply, but the team is doing everything possible to get everybody out of the motel and into somebody's spare bedroom.

"It's not because people think you're house-wrecking shit-asses or anything like that," the manager explains. "Becka can't even get taken in."

He tells them to fill out their W-2 forms and to be extra nice to Booster Club members and to never, ever refuse a little kid's autograph request.

"I don't care if he wants you to sign every page of his school notebook. You do it."

Then Shwam says there are three more days of training camp and there's plenty of work to be done and nobody should assume he has already made the team.

Having said that, Chris Cosbey has made the team.

The same politically incorrect thought runs through the mind of every Otter, regardless of race, creed or national origin: Cosbey is the fastest white boy they've ever seen.

Maybe 5-9. Maybe 160 pounds. Specialty is the drag bunt down third.

Cosbey takes his place on the left side of the batter's box and taps his bat against his cleats to remove any engine drag.

The third baseman wasn't born yesterday and comes up to the edge of the infield grass. But he doesn't stop there. He takes another step in. And another. And another until he's near enough to Cosbey that he can differentiate nose hairs.

The defender is smug. By God, the guy might kill him with a line drive, but no way he gets a bunt down.

Cosbey takes a strike, steps out and exhales. Because he is so close, the third baseman swats his breeze.

The pitcher sends the next pitch well outside and only a few inches off the ground. Cosbey shortens up on the bat handle and steers the ball toward the third-base bag as true as if he used a protractor. The fielder comes up with the ball cleanly. And why shouldn't he? I mean, he's right there. His throw across the diamond is perfect, not unlike Brooks Robinson in those grainy highlights.

The only problem is that Cosbey has already finished his forward momentum and is walking back to first.

This scenario has played out almost every day of training camp. The defense knows what's coming and still can't stop it.

"White lightning," somebody hollers as Cosbey brushes himself off on the bag.

"My car can't get down the line that fast," another says.

Cosbey smiles shyly. Anything else would be boastful. Anything else would suggest he is Mister High and Mighty RPMs and his teammates are horsepower-challenged. He won't go down that road at any speed.

What is really important isn't the compliments. It's taking second base. Two pitches later, he's there. Not wanting to waste his time, the catcher doesn't even cock his arm.

"My goal is 50 steals this season and to have fun with it," Cosbey says after the scrimmage. "Put the number in my hat. Draw a line through it every time I get one. Have a countdown to zero. Like a space launch."

At 26, he is one of the oldest Otters. This is his third season in professional ball. He played in the Northwest League and then in Modesto for the Oakland A's where he was released.

Cosbey is a substitute world history teacher at a high school outside Los Angeles where he helped coach the baseball team. He still lives with his parents.

"There was a lot of back-stabbing at Modesto," he says.

"Guys were openly rooting against teammates. They were afraid you'd get moved up and leave them behind. From what I've seen so far, independent league ball isn't like that. It's more pure baseball. You hope everybody gets picked up."

Keith Law is getting most of the grounders at shortstop. Drafted as a pitcher by Detroit, he came to the Otters to relearn how to play the infield. Tall, lanky and thin. Very thin. Says he weighs 175 pounds, but that would be holding a couple of medicine balls.

He empties one tin of snuff into his lip and starts in on a fresh container.

Most affiliated minor leagues ban the use of tobacco products. Not the Frontier League. You could stick a pound of burley between cheek and gum for all they care.

Law says pro teams have "dip patrols."

"You don't see them. They're in the stands or up in the pressbox. Their job is to look at what you put in your mouth. Somebody said they use binoculars. If it's chew or snuff, it's a $100 fine. They call you up after the game and you're busted."

Law says he goes to the snuff early and often because it keeps him from "going crazy" during games.

"At least I don't eat with it in there. I played with a guy once who'd throw down hamburgers, hot dogs, whatever, and the dip stayed right in place. People would stop what they were doing just to watch."

Overheard:

"Anybody seen the resin bag?

"Just get our nastiest player and rub off on him. Same thing."

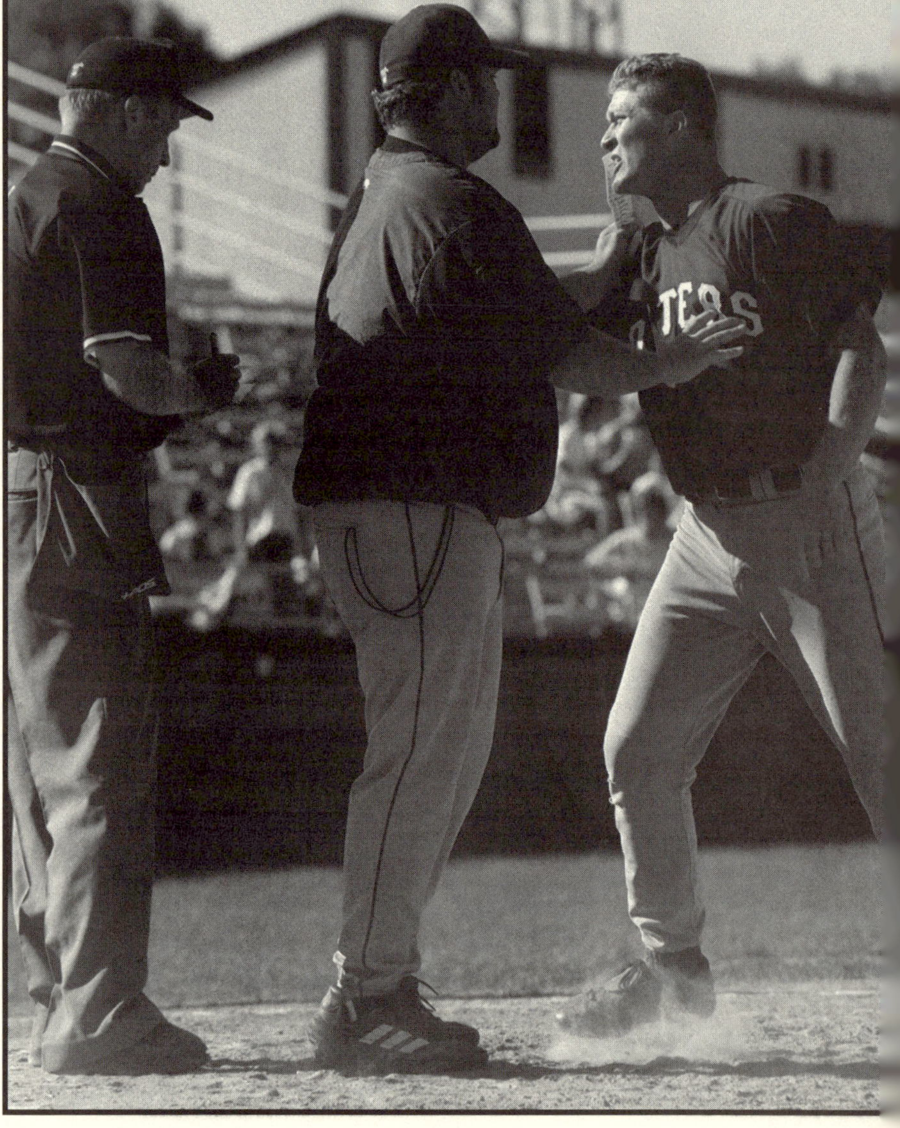

3

Getting to Know You

BILL BUSSING, 44, will be his family's main liaison with the Investment lawyer. Often called upon to be a fund raiser for civic projects. Weighs a trim 150. Looks like a younger Gene Wilder. Says he was a horrible baseball player as a kid. Says he struck out playing slow-pitch softball. Huge St. Louis Cardinals fan. Has listened to them on the radio since 1971. Arranges his schedule around their games. Takes a two-inch radio and an earpiece into meetings. Has never been to an Otters' game.

Say what?

"Oh, I knew the team was in town and everything, but it just never hit me to see them play," Bussing says. "The Goldklang Group put out a feeler that they might be interested in buying the team if there was the right local involvement. Marv (Goldklang) knew Charlie Jacey and knew that he wasn't doing well financially with the team. Marv believed the team was undercapitalized and could make money with a good management team.

"It sounded like fun, but I needed my family's backing. I presented it to them and maybe because I was so excited about doing something with baseball, they decided to go along.

"It wasn't something like if the Bussings don't do something, the team might leave town. The situation never was that desperate. I'm in the investment business. I became convinced that down the road we could come out ahead. When my picture got in the newspaper, I was, oh, wow, I finally made the sports section."

The Goldklang Group would not confirm the exact sales price, but Bussing says it was in the neighborhood of $600,000. The family had no part in the negotiations and will have only a consulting role in the team's management.

Bussing says owning part of a baseball team is not like having a fancy wind-up toy.

"Because that trivializes it. Whatever I set out to do, I try to do it well. Just because it's a fun venture doesn't mean it isn't a serious one. The interesting thing about all this is I don't have any idea what my role is. What does a 13-percent-share guy do on game night? Should I slap Dan Shwam on the back? Should I have personal relationships with the players? Should I help sell hot dogs? Should I stand on the dugout and be a cheerleader? I'll learn as I go."

MAY 30

Evansville's season begins as it will end—with three games against the Dubois County Dragons at Huntingburg, Ind.

These Otters have watched enough baseball movies to know they're getting a double shot of cinema lore.

Built in 1915, Bosse Field is one of the oldest ballparks in the country—so vintage, in fact, that it has a covered roof over much of the stands.

Sixty miles away, the Dragons play in a slightly smaller stadium that's equally retro with the roof thing.

In 1991, Hollywood was scouting locations for "A League of Their Own" about two female professional baseball teams during World War II. Bosse Field and Huntingburg Park, later renamed League Stadium, were selected because they most looked like ballyards that fit the time period.

Stars Tom Hanks, Madonna and Geena Davis spent that sweltering summer in woolen baseball jerseys on the closed sets that were the two ballparks.

During training camp, several Otters took pictures of each other in the corner of the dugout where Hanks' hung-over character tried to shield himself from the sun.

Upon arriving at League Stadium, a few players go straight from the bus to the hand-numbered scoreboard in left field and pose for snapshots.

"Pick up some grass and put it on eBay, dude," one suggests. "Make some money. Tell people it's where Madonna fell down."

There are foxholes bigger than the visiting team's one-urinal locker room. The 24 Otters and three coaches would have to be layered to fit. This is entirely too kinky to consider so early in the season, so some dress outside the door next to the gift shop.

Evansville's starting pitcher is Tom Miller of Kansas City, released from the Giants' organization after going 4-2 at Class A Bakersfield in 2000. Redhead. Freckles. Has degree in exercise psychology. Works in cardio-rehab with special-needs patients. Baseball traditionalist. Pulls his stirrups higher than anyone else on the team. Newly married. Ask his career goal and he'll say, "To get to know my wife."

He is the oldest of the pitchers at 26. And the wisest. Other hurlers pepper him with questions about everything from how to grip a slider to the best way to get stretched. Miller has his own training regimen which goes well beyond the conditioning prescribed by Carmichael. He even runs for 20 minutes behind the outfield fence after games he pitches.

"I throw in the low 80s," he says. "Lots of grounders to second base. If I strike anybody out, they should stop the game."

The Otters break out to a 8-1 lead after five innings. Brian

Harrison sits at the end of the bench holding his bat. The third baseman's face is more radiant than the Christ child's in the department store manger when the light bulb under the straw is turned on.

"It could end right here. I got a hit in pro ball."

Indeed he did. A double to the left-center gap that drove in two runs.

"A hit, dude, and they're gonna pay me for it. Shit, this is heaven."

Harrison, 23, is appearing in his first game since June of 2000, when he played for Shawnee State University in Ohio. He wasn't drafted. Three tryouts later that year with teams as far as away as Connecticut failed to produce a contract. He went to work at the family business, a steel storage facility in Cleveland, where he fit cables under the steel and drove a tow motor.

He's the biggest Otter at 225 pounds—and the slowest. It's like Harrison gave birth and Cosbey came out. He rolls with the jokes, saying not only is he overweight, he's pretty much worthless.

At first glance, you'd figure him for team clown. Always has some kind of secret handshake going. Pretends to feel Becka up before games for luck. Plays spirited games of "Touched You Last" on the bus. Asks batboys if they want some chew.

But down deep Harrison has a desperate desire to play, which is accompanied by an equally large dose of self-doubt.

Ask any Otter playing a power position his season goal and he'll say 10 home runs, 35 RBI and a ticket out of this place. This is how Harrison answered the question: "To not be the first cut at training camp."

The Otters' middle relievers falter in the late innings, giving up 4 runs. Huntingburg is a German enclave. Each time a Dragon reaches home, the PA breaks into a spirited "Roll Out the Barrel."

"Get them out, for Christ's sake," an annoyed Shwam hollers. "This ain't no damn brew hall."

Nick Stelzner isn't sure he's supposed to pitch the ninth. He stands at the bullpen mound with a quizzical look on his face.

Carmichael waves him into the game.

"Kids," he grumbles. "Have to tell 'em everything."

The strong-armed righty preserves the 8-5 victory. No more barrels.

"Yeah, yeah, yeah," Shwam exclaims after the last out as he shuffles out onto the field, grabbing hands and patting backs.

The players don't know what to make of this. It's like a distant relative they barely know who gets this sudden notion to pay a social call.

Most brush past without making eye contact. Their body language says, hey, pops, let us enjoy the first victory privately and we'll sort out this employee-employer business later.

Scott Suraci is the offensive star with a home run and a triple. He was released by the Minnesota Twins during spring training despite hitting .300. Says they had 13 outfielders so they gave up on him. Needs 27 credits for degree in finance. Wants to work for an investment firm and specialize in mutual funds.

That notwithstanding, he came to Evansville with $300 and is down to $35. He's told his brother to please wire $100 as soon as possible or he'll have to start hocking his protein bars.

Hawk-nosed. Scholarly. Reminds me of a young Sherlock Holmes with an outfielder's glove. Easy to like. Enjoys taking his two young cousins to the playground to hit. Tells me he would play baseball for a dollar. Then he remembers his off-field career and amends that to say he would play for cost-of-living expenses.

Has been a student of nutrition since high school. Heavy into supplements and amino acids. Never eats fast food. Says he rarely drinks beer and, when he does, it's just to be social.

Harrison can't believe he's hearing this. Fast food? He was weaned on it. And beer? He wishes it was in an IV bag when he comes off the field.

He downs an imaginary beaker and pretends to erect a barrier between himself and Suraci.

"Quit trying to infect me. Stay away."

Shortstop Keith Law pulled a hamstring at the end of camp. Backup Mike Butler will play the Dubois series.

Butler has the worst-looking goatee on the team. Starts strong on the right side, weakens substantially in the middle and then fizzles out altogether. Lives in Sonora, Cal., near Yellowstone National Park. Has a year left at Sacramento State College where he is majoring in communications. Works at Pac Bell putting up telephone poles. Earns $12 an hour digging the holes. Says he can make twice that much climbing the poles.

"I'm here to prop the other guys up," a wide-eyed Butler says. "To be a good guy in the clubhouse. I'm not kidding anybody. I'm just glad to be here. The season will be one life experience after another. See new things, you know? Like those green plants growing next to the highway we saw on the bus coming out here. Not corn. I know corn. What's that other stuff with the leaves hanging down like little willow trees?"

Soybeans. Indiana is crammed full of them.

"I'll learn soybeans, then," Butler says. "When I get back home, I'll tell my buddies. They'll think I'm shitting 'em. I'll say, 'No, man. Soybeans.'"

MAY 31

Dubois County is the only day trip on the schedule. Get to Bosse Field a little before 3. Take the gray and maroon uniform off the hanger in your locker and stuff it into your equipment bag along with bats, gloves, socks and spikes. Throw the bag into the hold of the bus. Find a seat. Make sure you haven't forgotten your cellphone. Put on the wrap-around shades, adjust the headphones, try to find a seat next to someone who has a PlayStation and you're ready to roll.

Group stretch begins as soon as everyone is dressed. Batting practice lasts from 4:30 until 5:15. Pitchers shag fly balls and pretend to be Roberto Clemente. Outfield and infield practice takes place after the home team's BP. Then the Otters have a few minutes to themselves while they change into their game jerseys. The oranges and apples come out along with the Power-Ade, although a few players patiently wait in the concession line for hot dogs.

The game will last until approximately 9:45, longer if the home plate umpire lets each batter step out of the box after each pitch and stretch every muscle group the way the arbiter did on opening night.

Then it will be a fast rinse-off or even none at all, because the Dubois shower room has foot fungus written all over it.

Allowing for a food stop, the bus should be back at Bosse Field before midnight. Most host families live within a few miles of the ballpark, but some players have to drive to the next county before they can finally sack out.

"Some people think we show up at the field a few minutes before the game and then right after the last out, some genie snaps her fingers and we're tucked in bed," B. J. Richter says. "It makes me laugh."

The Otters open up a 4-0 lead behind Cliff Brand, who pitches seven shutout innings.

Inside the dugout, it sounds like this.

"Becka, dude, come over here and stretch me out. My hammy is tighter than a motherfucker."

"Hey, tank, stand in front of the trash can. Something fucking died in there, man. You can block the smell."

"Check out this zit, dude. Two hairs in one hole."

"C'mon, blue, he's quick-pitching us, goddammit."

"Who stole my fucking sunflower seeds? What do I have to do—staple them to my ass?"

"Look at the rack on that bitch in the second row, dude. Bet she's got a pussy bigger than the zero on the scoreboard."

"You know how they always say how a fly ball was a can of corn? Why couldn't it be a bowl of brown beans?"

"One time I won 500 dollars at the craps table at Tahoe."

"You're shitting me, dude."

"Couldn't believe it. Money was coming down like goddamn rain."

"Quit farting, man. You got to do that shit, go up in the runway."

Which brings us to Jeremy Coronado, a rookie outfielder who hit .352 his last year at Pepperdine University.

Small. Quiet. Intense. Deeply religious. Says he wants to win souls for God's kingdom. Says every day he is more on fire for the Lord. Says God delivered him nine months ago from the bondage of sin.

How bad was he before that?

"We went to Tijuana. I broke the commandments."

What would he be doing if he wasn't sitting in a dugout in Huntingburg, Ind.?

"Being a witness to God in the streets."

Why isn't he a minister?

"I enjoy being in the battlefield."

Has he shared his "Go, God" feelings with teammates?

"Yes. I love these guys. I don't want them to live in wickedness and be sent to hell."

How do they react?

"Some of them don't like it."

The Otters have no one in the on-deck circle, a violation that is pointed out by the plate umpire.

"Who's fucking hitting next?" somebody hollers.

"Look at the lineup card, you dumb-shit moron," somebody replies.

Coronado looks deep into my eyes.

"What is your personal relationship with Jesus Christ, Our Lord and Savior?" he wants to know.

Uh, well, er . . .

He presses the point.

"Can you tell me right here, right now, that you are ready for the Hereafter?"

Gee, Jeremy, there's a game going on.

"We have to answer for every idle word. God could come take us this instant."

In the middle of an inning?

"Goddammit, Coronado, you're up," someone says.

He breaks off the conversation, grabs his bat and races to the plate. He takes two balls outside, then cracks a line drive that bounces against the right-field wall.

The dugout is in collective awe. Coronado wasn't even half ready and he smoked a rope. Maybe there is something to the Holy Trinity.

Josh Hudson has won the starting catcher's job. One of the youngest guys on the team at 22. Played for the Adirondack Lumberjacks in the Northern League last year. Asked for a guarantee that he would get 250 at-bats if he came back. The team said no, so Hudson walked. Shwam believes he will hit better than Brandon Mattingly.

Hudson and Mattingly couldn't be more different.

Hudson is fastidious about his appearance. Every article of clothing must be just right. Need someone to model your new line of unis? Here's your guy. Deep tan. Boyish good looks. Mattingly is terminally scruffy. Everything he puts on looks like it has been through a shredder.

Hudson's shin guards, mask and chest protector represent the gold standard of a catcher's outerwear. Mattingly's battered gear looks like it was stolen from the Babe Ruth League.

Hudson does not cuss. "Gol-dang it" is as far as he goes. Mattingly can take the verb "to fuck" and through sheer force of will can take it to grammatical plateaus unreached even by champions of the lexicon.

Cosbey comes up to bat.

Normally a serious time. A time of intense concentration. A time to pick up the speed, direction and spin of the ball as quickly as possible so you don't receive the same ugly welt on your forearm that Jewell Williams did the night before.

Mattingly gets to the edge of the dugout and comes full-throat.

"Flex your nuts out there."

Cosbey steps out. The teacher in him grins as he looks at Mattingly. That was too good. Anybody can holler out the archaic "C'mon, babe," or "Get a little bingle" or "Put some wood on it." But flexing one's nuts as an implicit comparison for trying to get a base knock? That's a major league metaphor. Bravo.

The Otters go on to win, 4-1, but the big news is that Becka is caught spitting sunflower seeds.

"Next is chewing," Keith Law predicts. "Just a matter of time."

JUNE 2

Opening night in Evansville draws a near-capacity crowd of more than 5,200 fans.

The pitchers are so excited to see all the people they forget who has dibs on what they call "the stim machine." It is by far the most popular item in Becka's black bag. Ibuprofen isn't even a close second.

Brad Love shows how it works.

"Wires run to these two pads that you hook to your arm. It stimulates the muscles with an electric shock. Don't want to get too much. I usually set it on around 4."

It looks as if Love's arm is listening to music.

"They say it helps get the lactic acid out," the lefty says. "I don't know. Probably just a mental thing. But if everybody else is doing it, you don't want to be left out."

Love pitched at the University of Tennessee. Played last year in the Texas-Louisiana League. Will be given a chance to start for the Otters. Shwam says Love has some of the best stuff on the team, but that he tries to overanalyze everything.

"Sometimes when I pitch I really believe I'm on my way," Love says. "I go to bed thinking, man, I'm pretty good. Then the next time I don't have a thing. I need to be strong enough to battle through those games, but so far I'm not. Somebody makes an error and I think the guy would have made the play if so-and-so was on the mound."

I check out the Bosse Field dugout where I'm going to be spending a lot of time this summer.

Cramped, particularly when players leave gloves, hats and shin guards on the bench. And hot. Very hot. The air reaches the top of the dugout and starts to come in. Then it gets a whiff of the chew and snuff that's commingled with the sunflower seeds, slams on the brakes and takes off in the opposite direction.

Even with the thin layer of rubber spread over the concrete, it's about as comfortable as a Calvinist church pew. You have to get up every few minutes or risk atrophy to your hind parts.

Brian Harrison pulled a quad in the Dubois series, which means playing time for fellow rookie Chris Adams. Adams is small, but powerfully built. Has one of the best arms on the team and can even pitch in an emergency. Says he once broke a rib when hit by a pitch but stayed in the game. Says Shwam may have him pegged as a utility man, but that's not the way he sees it.

"I didn't come here to sit the bench," Adams maintains.

Eric Cooper holds Springfield scoreless for six innings. Like Cliff Brand's, his fastball isn't the greatest, but he mixes his pitches well and throws strikes.

The Otters get 11 hits, including another home run by Suraci, but lose 6-5 when Springfield rallies late. It's Evansville's first loss.

Andy Miller comes out to put the tarp over the mound.

"When Shwam asked me into his office, I thought he was going to give me a contract," Miller says as he cleans the pitching rubber. "He told me I wasn't polished enough to help him at second base and he said he has enough outfielders. Then, boom, released."

Will he try to play again?

"No, I'd say this is it."

Was it embarrassing for the players to see him like this— you know, dirtbagging?

"A little. When I got here today, I looked in the dugout and was kinda hoping nobody would be there. But I talked with a couple of the guys and it's OK now."

What if Shwam asked him to stay ready in case somebody gets hurt?

"I've got too much pride for that. If I can't make the team, I'm not going to be some kind of sub."

JUNE 3

Nolan Fry asks if I remember Kim Batiste.

Sure. Shortstop for the Phillies in the 1993 World Series against Toronto.

"Well, I got him out," he says proudly.

In 1998, Batiste was trying to make a comeback and joined the Allentown, Pa., entry in the Northern League. Fry was pitching for the Catskill, N.Y., team.

"Comebacker. I made a nice play and threw him out at first. Later that night, I drank beer and shot pool with him. He was like a regular guy. That's as close as I've ever been to the top."

Fry pitched the last two seasons for Dubois—mostly out of the bullpen—and has a combined 10-1 record.

He knows all his numbers. Pitched in 31 of 84 games. Has an ERA of 3.08. Has 99 strikeouts. Has allowed 49 walks in 94 innings.

How can he keep track of all that?

"If a teacher was telling me something like that in school, I'd forget. But it's baseball, so I remember. It's not bragging or anything. If a cross-checker asks, I want to be able to tell him."

Fry says there are two scouts he calls after each appearance.

"It's not some bogus, 'How ya doing?' stuff," he says defensively. "The one guy drove two hours in February to watch me pitch for 20 minutes."

He shows me his cap that has "Location," "No Mercy" and "No Fear" printed on it in big, black letters.

"Keys to victory," Fry explains. "I keep them as close to my brain as possible."

Evansville scores 8 in the fourth and goes up 11-3 on its way to a 12-6 win.

The mood is light in the dugout in the late innings.

Roe: "Britt says I have to run a pole for every beer. Babe Ruth drank beer all the time. How much did he run?"

Williams: "Don't be bringing that religious shit around me."

Cooper: "If the other team forfeits, which pitcher gets the win? The manager should get to choose, don't you think?"

Butler: "I can root for the guy who plays my position, but deep down I want him to do shitty."

Miller: "What I need more than anything is a good foot deodorizer."

Mattingly: "Game's not over yet. Let's get some more shit up on the board."

Love sneezes.

Coronado: "God bless you."

JUNE 5

The left-handed hitter hits a two-hopper up the middle. The second baseman stabs the ball and throws across his body.

The first base ump raises his fist and snaps it down hard to sell the close call.

The player's face turns red and then twists in anger. The helmet is taken off the head with both hands and slammed into the ground where it is kicked halfway to home plate.

Mark Thomas has made an out.

He hates it when that happens.

Thomas mutters obscenities all the way back to the dugout. He picks his bat up and holds it over his head like a spear.

"Oh, shit," Cooper says. "Right fielder madman on the loose. Dude's gonna take us out."

Everybody moves away from that side of the dugout. A couple of guys even go up the runway toward the clubhouse.

"Fuck," Thomas shouts.

The proper way to return a batting helmet is to place it carefully inside one of a dozen square cubicles next to the bat rack. Thomas throws his in there at 60 miles per hour. It shoots straight out and does a Mexican hat dance on the floor of the dugout before finally coming to rest.

"Fuck. Fuck. Fuck."

The words come out like an automatic weapon.

"Just three more fucking inches and I've got a hit. Is that too fucking much to ask?"

Nobody is anywhere near the guy.

What would you say?

"Uh, gee, Mark, from our angle it looked like you were only out by one inch."

Or:

"Golly, Mark, factor in gravitational forces and the Earth's rotation on its axis and you were safe by a step. We'll go to the nearest science lab first thing tomorrow and file a protest."

Nick Stelzner is pursuing a graduate degree in psychology. Cliff Brand says figuring Thomas out should be worth at least a doctorate.

Stelzner shakes his head.

"That would mean being in the same room with him."

You can always use restraining devices, Brand suggests.

"Maybe then," Stelzner says, "but only then."

Thomas plays even more balls-out than Mattingly. Earlier in the series, the Springfield catcher had to be helped off the field after Thomas ran over him as he scored from second on a single to left.

"Mark has the strongest will to win of any kid I've seen in a long time," Shwam says. "Most guys say, 'Shit, I'm not going to kill myself on every at-bat. It's a long season, man. I'm going to take it easy running out that ground ball.' Thomas isn't like that. Each play to him is like the end of the world. You make the play if you want to live.

"I know he throws stuff and shit, but that's OK if you're mad at yourself and you're not blaming somebody else. And he can run for a 200-pounder. Cosbey and Coronado steal because they're fast. Thomas steals because the middle infielders know he'll take them out. I'll say this. The way he plays, Thomas hits .300 and he's out of here (to an affiliated club)."

The skies, which have been threatening all night, explode in the third inning. Within minutes, there's standing water in the dugout. The grounds crew-composed of every non-player in the Otters' employ—comes from the front office, the ticket booths, the concession stands and the souvenir shop to pull the tarp over the infield. They do their best, but the rain has already formed a trench between second and third.

Harrison allows that it would be fun to dive on the tarp.

"Go for it, dude," Cooper exhorts. "Put a pillow over your stomach."

"But what if there's something in the Frontier League rulebook?" Harrison says. "Thou shalt not fart around on the field during quagmires."

The home plate umpire overhears.

"I will if you will."

"No shit?" Harrison asks.

"Why not?" the ump replies. "Give the fans a laugh."

"Do it," Scott Suraci says. "Rain delays are boring. It's not like the people have television sets out in the stands. We've got to entertain our public."

"Then *you* get out there," Harrison counters.

"But you're built perfectly for this," Suraci argues. "Go face first. That Budweiser gut will take the blow. You're always joking around. Be right in character for you to make an ass out of yourself."

Brian Harrison sits back in the dugout. He is suddenly serious. His mind is made up. No belly-flopping.

"Shwam might cut me. I'm probably on the edge as it is. Do something he doesn't like and I'm gone."

Teammates continue to egg on Harrison. Cooper even turns the guy's cap sideways, the precursor in the tableau of baseball that tomfoolery is about to take place.

Harrison walks away without speaking.

What started as a joke isn't one any more. He takes a seat at the other end of the dugout and looks out onto the field. Just the hint of end game has him thinking about the time—days, weeks or months from now—when he won't have a baseball uniform to put on and that makes him want to be alone.

Mark Thomas, 25, has a year left to get his degree at Youngstown (Ohio) State. Drafted in the 21st round, this is his third year as a pro.

"I was released in the second week of spring training by the Expos," he says. "The clubbie took my pants out of my locker. That's how I found out. I went into the manager's office and cried like a baby for 20 minutes. I know I can play Double-A. Shit, I know I can play Triple-A. I kept begging him to take me back like I was some kid on the playground and he wouldn't let me on the monkey bars any more. It was the absolute worst day of my life.

"That day I called all 29 big-league organizations. My cellphone bill was outrageous. I kept getting told the same thing: no jobs. All the teams were dumping their high-round players so they could play their top draft picks. Guys like me get hung out to dry. We might be better than the players they took in the second and third rounds, but we don't get the chance. They pay those shits the big bucks. No matter how much they suck, they're gonna be in the lineup."

I tell him I've never seen anybody play with such a rage.

"That's a strong word, rage. I'd call it desire. That's why it hurt so bad to be released. I did everything they said. Extra BP. Extra fly balls. They could have told me to come to the park five hours early and I'd say, sure, no problem. I'll sleep here if you want me to."

I ask Thomas what he'll do when he stops playing.

"The degree I'm working on is communications. Maybe chase sports stories with a camera. No money in it, but no money here either. I've got this elastic stretch thing that I use before games to get loose. Works real good. Maybe I could go on the road and help the guy sell them."

He looks out at the rain.

"That's all bullshit. The truth is, I never want baseball to be over."

Jewell Williams has already been hit four times around the elbow. Shwam worries about his reaction time.

"It's like the ball is coming in on him and he's thinking oh, shit, now what do I do? By the time he comes up with an answer, he's plunked."

Shane Smuin sits quietly by the Gatorade cooler, rubbing his wedding ring.

Released by the Florida Marlins. Works construction in the off-season. Would rather talk about his wife than baseball.

"Meagan is a real trouper. When I think of all she has had to put up with so I can play, it makes me want to bow down to her.

"Last season, I was like a human moving van. Utah to Florida. Then Chicago. Then Florida again. Then to Utica, New York, where I lived in the team dorm. I pitch five innings. No runs allowed. Get sent down. I pitch four innings. No runs. Get sent down."

This year with the Otters will be a financial nightmare.

"My idea was for my wife and I to live with a host family in

Evansville. That didn't work out, so we had to get an apartment at $650 a month. That's a hundred dollars less than my salary."

Smuin says his father is the "agent guy."

"I'm his dream. He's all the time calling affiliated teams and if there's even a sprig of interest, he sends my stats. I'm really lucky to have him helping me."

I ask Coronado about his religious conversion, to go back to when he was breaking the commandments.

"In high school, I always wanted to do things right and follow the Lord. But when I went away to college, I became that very person I despised as a youth. God was always knocking on my heart to turn from that stuff, but I took too much pleasure in my sins. I used to feel horrible about myself when I would get drunk and sleep with girls I barely knew. I knew I wasn't walking in the will of God.

"I wasn't drafted after my 2000 season at Pepperdine and I lost my passion for baseball. I still had a semester left in school. I didn't know whether to keep pursuing the game or finish classes and start working. It was at the end of that summer that God changed my life completely. I was tired of feeling shameful and the Lord gave me the gift of repentance, which completely changed my heart.

"That renewed my desire to play ball. I started training and knew that the Lord would open a door for me to play. The Otters offered me a contract and I came to spring training. I've been blessed with the year I've had so far and to be able to witness to my teammates."

The Otters go 3-2 on the homestand against Springfield and Cook County. Add the wins in Huntingburg and they're 6-2.

At Bosse Field, the coaches hang out in what amounts to a large rec room with a couple of toilets and pipes going every which way. On the floor are broken bats, McDonald's wrappers, boxes of baseballs, dirty socks and what is left of a Mennen Speed Stick. Nobody ever picks anything up.

Shwam has a desk, two chairs, a phone, a stack of pencils, a calendar and a bulletin board. Carmichael has a chair and a desk. Brown and Ryan share a sofa and a coffee table.

I tell the skip that Harrison and a few other players are scared to death they're going to be released.

"Insecure?" he says.

Yes, that's the word.

The manager shrugs his shoulders.

"Insecurity is part of independent league baseball. Nobody's safe for the rest of the season, not even me. I tell them they've always have a spot on this team and they'll say 'Hot damn' and relax and then they'll go zip-for-40 or, if they're a pitcher, they'll start rolling the ball up to the plate.

"I don't want to cut guys, but you know what they say—shit runs downhill. If the players want to keep things the way they are, they need to win. We put a streak together and I'll stick with the guys I have."

And if they lose?

"You know the revolving door that you see in hotels? Well, they'll have to install one outside Bosse Field."

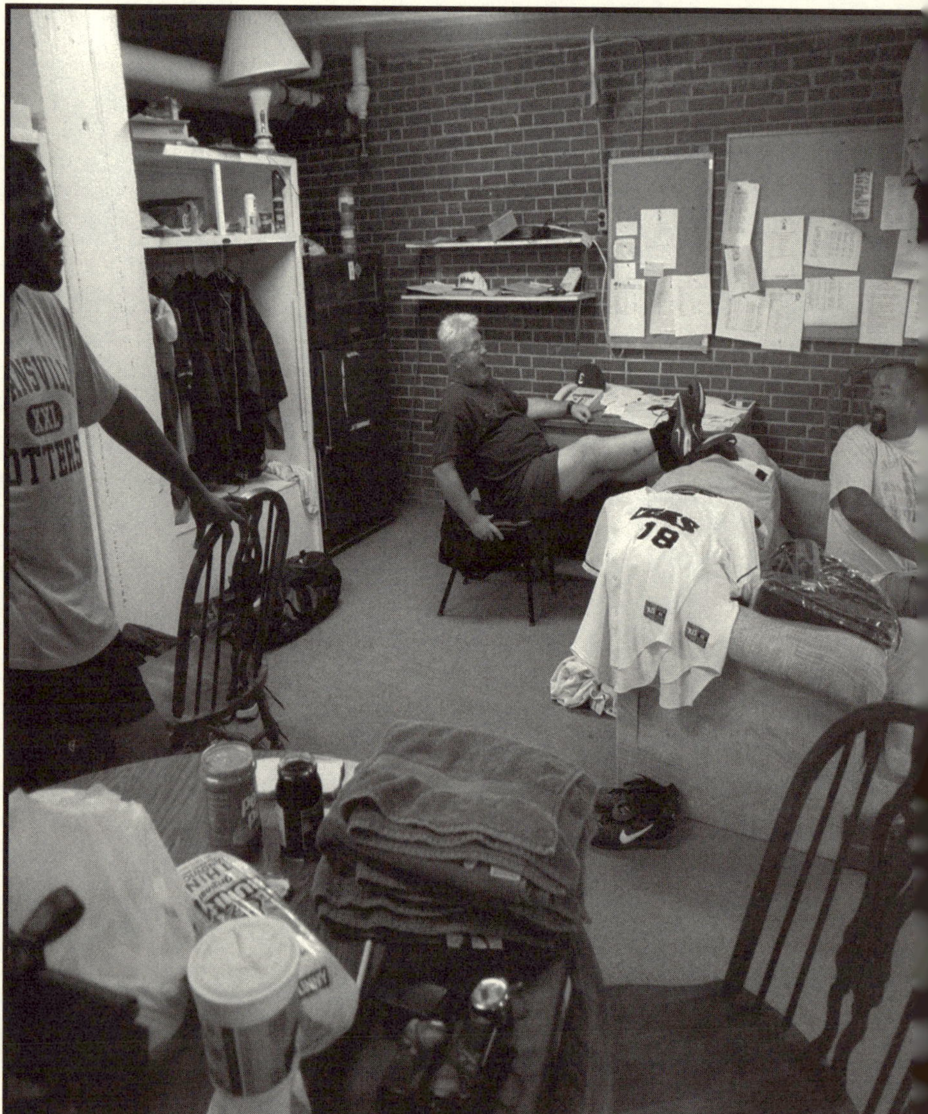
OTTERS
18

4

I Went In Like It Was Death

JEWELL WILLIAMS hits a home run in the top of the sixth to give the Otters a 2-1 lead over River City.

He watches every moment of it. The launch. The flight. The landing. Only then does Williams take his turn around the bases and he does it at the speed of a second-grade girl skipping to Grandma's house. The other team isn't amused.

"He's pimping it big time," Chris Adams observes. "He'd better watch out."

Williams comes up again in the eighth. The first pitch almost brains him. Todd Brown runs to the mound, hollering to the umpire that he saw the River City coach signal for a beaning. The next pitch follows the same flight plan. Williams throws his bat at the pitcher. The benches clear, but the umpires jump in the middle like MPs outside a servicemen's club and order is restored.

Williams and Shwam are ejected. River City's field has no runway, so security guards escort the pair through the stands to the bus.

In the bottom of the inning, Terry Roe throws his first pitch at the hitter's adenoids and is ejected. Another forced promenade through the stands to the bus.

Smuin and Stelzner do not allow a baserunner in the last three innings. The Otters win in 10 innings on a sacrifice fly by Thomas.

"What Roe did was not smart, not smart at all," Shwam says after the game. "I told him not to retaliate. After they kicked my ass out, I made sure Britt told him not to retaliate. We're damn lucky there wasn't a huge fight."

Jewell Williams says his bat "sorta slipped."

Would he throw it again under the same circumstances?

"Yes. Dude don't need to be throwing at my head."

Brian Harrison is back in the lineup at third base.

I ask if his quad has healed.

"No way. I don't tell Shwam. I don't tell Becka. The team's already given me seven days. That's all I'm gonna get. If I can't play, they'll send me home."

Harrison is thrown out trying to get to third from second on a fly ball to deep right. The play isn't close.

Carmichael to Nolan Fry: "You're rushing out there on the mound."

Fry: "Am I rushing my upper body or my lower body?"

Carmichael: "I don't know. They're connected."

JUNE 12

The Otters weigh in with their thoughts on the playing conditions at Sauget, Ill., home of the Gateway Grizzlies.

Chris Cosbey: "There are gopher holes in the outfield. I wouldn't put my high school team on it. The steel sprinkler heads are showing. The infield grass is so thick Harrison could beat out a grounder."

Mark Thomas: "Thoroughly crappy. If the league cared about its players, we wouldn't be here. Worst lights I've ever seen. Guy hit a ball my way and I absolutely could not track it. The first time I saw it was when it hit the ground 15 feet from me. Ridiculous. Totally ridiculous."

Dan Shwam: "A glorified American Legion field. They said they spent $200,000 to upgrade it. I sure don't see where the money went. And that tent shit is a joke."

He refers to the visitors' dressing room down the right field foul line. No toilet. No shower. Two picnic tables to sit on to get dressed. Gravel for a floor. The players put their clothes in piles like a bunch of little kids who are camping out.

Nick Stelzner comes in to close the game with the Otters leading, 4-3, going to the bottom of the ninth. Three walks, two hits and an error later, Evansville loses, 5-4 in 10 innings. The winning hit is a bloop to right field.

Stelzner throws his glove and stares into Gateway's dugout. When somebody hollers something back to him, he shares an F-bomb about how does it feel to hit a ball with a purse.

Blown save.

JUNE 13

Nolan Fry leaves with a 2-1 lead. Gateway scores two off Brad Steele in the eighth and wins, 3-2.

Blown save.

Jeremy Coronado, who is hitting over .400, hurts his shoulder running into the outfield fence. Because there is no warning track, he hits it full-bore.

JUNE 14

The game is tied 5-5 after nine innings when gale-force winds arrive. Tornado sirens go off. Lightning slices through the sky. Rain comes down hard enough to break the skin. The Otters retreat to their tent.

Which blows away.

JUNE 15

Second baseman Mike Butler makes two errors in one inning. A 4-1 Otters lead is erased and Johnstown goes on to a 9-6 victory.

"Yeah, I heard the boos," Butler says after the game. "There were people hollering that Shwam should have taken me out in the middle of the inning."

Butler is hitting around .100. Fielding is his strong suit. If he has problems doing that . . .

"It's bye-bye, I know. But you can't think like that. Shwam knows I'm good in the clubhouse. He knows I can play any position in the infield. I've got three sacrifice bunts and I wore a pitch the other night to get on base. He looked over at me from third and raised his fist, so he knows what I did."

Roe is released.

Suraci is striking out a lot.

Thomas and Williams have a heated exchange. Williams says he's tired of the people ahead of him in the lineup making outs. Thomas gets in his face and says look out for your own fucking batting average and leave me alone.

The shouting match doesn't come to blows, but more than one Otter tells me it was good to see someone stand up to Shwam's five-star player.

Becka says she finds herself doing girlie things like shopping and fixing her hair.

"It's not that I really want to," she says, "but I want to feel as different from the players as possible."

Two women approach Nick Stelzner after the game and suggest he party at their place.

"It's not something you'd rule out if they were good-looking. I mean, hey. But these chicks were sloppy drunk and, besides, it was on a get-away day. I just said, see you later, and went to the bus."

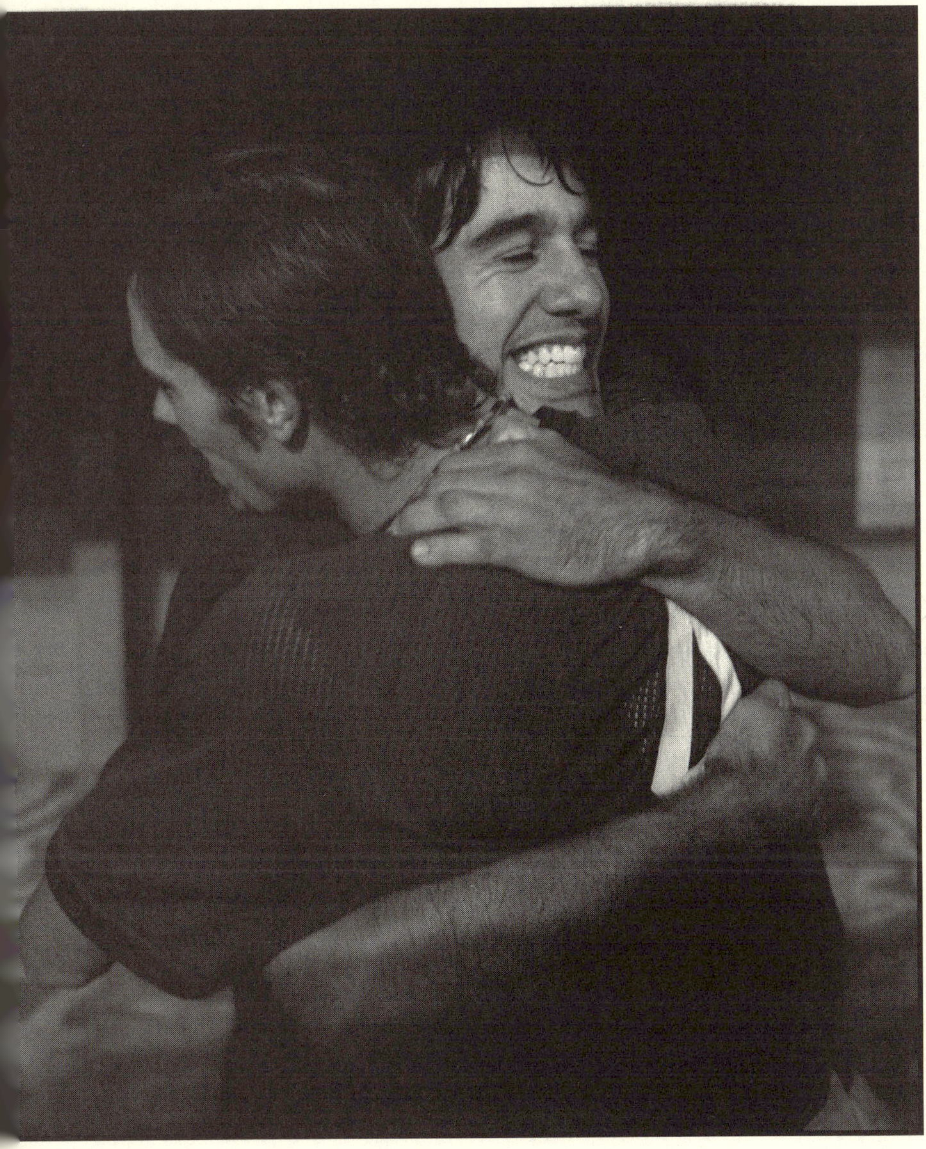

Ron Ryan spits and says he'd like to manage on this level some day, but he wouldn't even think of doing it until he coaches long enough to have a Rolodex full of potential players.

"You might be a genius between the lines," Ryan says, "but you've got to know where the studs are if you want to win."

Britt Carmichael spits and admits he's learning this pitching coach business as he goes along. He gets the feeling Shwam wants him to make more decisions, but he doesn't want to suggest a move that turns out wrong, so he clams up.

No player or coach with the Otters can talk for five minutes without the words "baseball gods" coming up at least once.

But Jeremy Coronado always corrects the blasphemers.

"There are no baseball gods. Just the one true Lord, our savior."

And there's another phrase that seems to come out of everyone's mouth.

You're supposed to be cool in baseball. Calm. Collected. Surprised by nothing.

And these guys are cool.

Attila the Hun could pinch-hit for Brian Harrison. He could rope the ball down third where Madame Curie makes a diving stop and throws across the diamond to Paul McCartney, the first baseman. But the ball is overthrown and brains the umpire, Rasputin, who tumbles into the bullpen where he is rescued by the ace closer, Lazarus.

Shwam and the others would roll their eyes and say, "Well, that's baseball."

JUNE 16

Susan Wargel and her husband, Steven, have hosted Otters for four seasons. Their son, Andy, is one of the batboys.

This year, they were assigned Brad Love.

"Our friends ask how in the world we can open up our home to somebody we don't know," she says. "I tell them they should come over and watch Nick Stelzner play gentle songs on his guitar and listen to Brad bow his head and say he owes his baseball career to God. They should meet Brad's girlfriend, Crystal, and get to know his mother who has driven up from Montgomery, Alabama, I don't know how many times to watch him play.

"You never know what's going to happen. One night, Keith Law got locked out of his host family's house and came over here. He acted like we were the nicest people in the world for letting him stay the night. He kept saying over and over again, 'I don't want to put you out. I don't want to put you out.' We just looked at him and said, 'Go down in the basement and get some sleep, for goodness sake.'"

Lisa Rust has started a Home Page on the Internet for her three Otters. She often spends an hour or more a day scanning in photographs and typing in newspaper interviews and game stories.

"I expected to have so-called regular guys at my house," she says. "You know who I'm talking about. Males who take over the couches and the television and leave trails of dirty clothes from room to room.

"This is absolutely not the case with my summer sons. Unless they're fixing something to eat, they hole up in their room for hours at a time. For a while, I worried that my house isn't comfortable to them. Then I realized everything's fine and that they're behaving like this because they just don't want to be in the way. It took shy little Jeremy the longest time to ask permission to cover the vents in the room because they were freezing."

JUNE 17

The Otters fall to 8-8 after losing, 1-0 to Canton. Cliff Brand fans a hitter, but Brandon Mattingly can't handle the third strike in the dirt and makes a wild throw to first, allowing the run to score from second.

In his first post-game tirade of the season, Shwam says the team is playing with no heart and guys who aren't producing will be shipped out.

JUNE 18

I ask pitcher Brad Love to name a leader on the team.

He thinks for a few seconds and shakes his head.

"We haven't earned each other's friendship," Love says. "You have to have that before you can talk about having leaders. It's like a nickname. You can't just decide on something. The others have to give it to you."

Shwam doesn't talk enough, Love says.

"He stands in the dugout with the other coaches and nobody knows what he's thinking. This makes guys play tight and that's when you make mistakes."

Cosbey says some of the younger players have complained to him about not getting any coaching.

"They feel Shwam should take the time to show them what they're doing wrong. They think there's no learning going on, just the games. They want a personal touch."

Chris Adams hits a three-run homer, his first of the season. He follows it the next time up with a solo shot. The third baseman comes into the dugout pumping his fists like a fighter. He makes it a point to find me.

"See, I told you I didn't come here to play backup," he says.

I ask Stelzner to name a leader.

"Miller, definitely. His work habits and how he's always helping somebody else. No ego. No attitude. He just wants to do all the right things to get better. The pitchers rely on him a lot more than Britt.

"And Chris Cosbey of the position players. He doesn't lord it over the other guys that he's so fast and so good at the top of the order. He doesn't yell. He just does what he's supposed to do and sits down like he's no more important than the bat boy."

Jewell Williams is at the plate. He takes a fastball for a strike, waves at two curves and about-faces to the dugout. It's a pattern that has been repeating more and more often. Throw him a breaking ball and Williams swings like a fencer with a broken pelvis.

Then he takes the at-bat to his position, almost walking to left field. Guys hustle more than this on their way to the electric chair.

"You were talking about leaders," Stelzner says, looking at the same mini-gait. "I don't think so."

Eric Cooper pitches five innings of shutout ball. He doesn't ask to be lifted, but doesn't complain either.

"My shoulder is tightening up," he tells Carmichael. "I'll give you nine innings next time."

Coronado still isn't in the lineup. Says his shoulder is hurt.

Shwam doesn't buy it, at least not completely.

"I've had a guy go through the wall—I mean, through it—and come back the next night, broken nose and all. I won't say it for a fact, but it could be that Jeremy is protecting his .400 average. He's small, almost fragile. That could hurt him down the road. Organized ball has tunnel vision when it comes to injuries. Is the guy strong enough to play 162 games? That's what they want to know. I love Jeremy as a person, but right now I couldn't put him on that list."

It's a satisfying evening. The Otters win, 9-3, over Canton, the best team in the Eastern Division.

The players talk about what they would do if they hit a walk-off-the-field home run in the bottom of the ninth.

"Pimp it every inch of the way around the bases and then retire," says Josh Hudson.

JUNE 19

Lightning and storms force the umpires to call the game against Chillicothe. Tomorrow will be interminable for the team. The rained-out game will be resumed in the top of the fourth. The regularly scheduled contest will follow. Then the Otters get on the bus for the 12-hour push to Johnstown, Pa.

Shwam bunks at an Evansville motel. He is at the park by 1 P.M., sometimes earlier.

His office telephone rings constantly.

"I get at least 30 calls a day from players and their agents. Guys are like vultures. They look at the Otters' web site and tell me they can hit better than that .150 piece of crap my second baseman is putting up. I say, 'Yeah, maybe you can, but I like what my second baseman does on the field and in the clubhouse.'

"Then I have the calls from management telling me about so-and-so player in Florida, or wanting to know why Jewell Williams isn't hitting, or wanting to know why I can't find a decent closer. The players have no idea about all this. They think all I do in here is wash my face."

He picks up the receiver.

"Fax me your stats, OK? I'll take a look. Have your coach call, too. That couldn't hurt."

Why not let the players in on this aspect of your job? I suggest after he puts the phone down. Let them know how you're fending off unemployed ballplayers out there who want their jobs. It might make them appreciate you more.

"Knowing I get all the phone calls would just put them under more stress. Let them think I've got my feet up. I don't want to make it harder on them than it already is."

He grins.

"It's my way of taking one for the team."

Hey, what's this from the allegedly unfeeling, unrelenting hammer? Is the armor cracking?

"Nobody roots harder for these kids than I do. I'm with them night and day. Shit, I'm a human being. You build up an attachment. You don't want to be the one who breaks up the family."

I thought I was the only one who had a growing reservoir of sentimentality for these guys. I understand how much the game means to them and how heartbroken they would be if told to clean out their lockers. Even though I've only known them a few weeks, I would feel a portion of that pain.

Shwam picks up the receiver.

"Can't make any promises, guy. You stay ready. You keep throwing. Might be something here for you down the road."

There must be something about talking to a left-handed pitching prospect that sends a manager hurtling back to the real world.

"The disappointing performance of this team can't be ignored. Williams, Suraci, Thomas—the middle of the lineup isn't driving in runs. Pretty soon, I'm going to have to give up on these guys. Call 'em in here and say I'm sorry it didn't work out.

"That's by far the hardest part of my job. Even the host families get involved. They liked the kid I had to let go. Will they get along as well with the new guy?"

Shwam picks up the receiver.

"Hey, babe, nothing has changed since you called yesterday. I haven't forgotten. Stay in touch, OK?"

He wipes his glasses.

"I would love to come in here at 4 o'clock, write out the lineup, talk to the players, find out how they're feeling, enjoy their company. But it's just not realistic. If I did that, I'd never have a minute to myself. The job would just eat me up."

He says no affiliated teams have inquired about any of his players. If he could pick one to move out, it would be Tom Miller.

"Great gentleman. Great worker. He knows the drill. He's not concerned with what I'm doing, only with what he's doing."

The word was that last year Greg Tagert earned $30,000 for his summer in Evansville.

"That's not my salary. Nowhere near. That kind of money is for a full-time guy. You want to know the truth, when I try to maintain two households, I actually lose money coming to Evansville.

"Managing in professional baseball is all Tagert does. I teach and coach high school for a living. Greg's approach to getting players is altogether different from mine. He's got all the time in the world. He hears about a prospect and can make arrangements to see him play. Me, I've got to rely on what a coach or a scout tells me. That definitely puts me behind the 8-ball."

Then why manage? Take a summer job selling insurance.

"I love the time I'm on a baseball field almost like one of my children. There's nothing that could be better. The shit starts before the game and picks up after the game, but for the two-and-a-half hours when the result is up for grabs, I'm the happiest person in the universe."

JUNE 20

The Otters lose, 9-3 and 5-1. The bus doesn't leave for Pennsylvania until almost midnight.

JUNE 21-26

The bussie gets lost trying to find Johnstown. Not the stadium. The city.

Players don't check into their motel rooms until early afternoon, getting only a couple hours of sleep before leaving for the stadium at 3 P.M.

Miller and Richter—who must have their eyelids taped open—combine on a seven-hitter and the Otters win the first game of the series, 7-2.

The next night, the bullpen blows a late 3-2 lead and Evansville loses, 5-3.

Jewell Williams goes hitless in both games.

"I should have eight or 10 home runs," Williams says. "I'm hitting too many balls foul. I need to be more patient."

What about the curve ball?

"I'm not trusting my hands. I'm too anxious to swing through the ball."

You've had more professional experience than any other Otter. Shouldn't you be a leader?

"Not when I'm going bad."

Butler buys at least a few more days on the team with two hits as Evansville scores eight runs in the seventh en route to a 12-3 pasting of Canton.

Cooper gives up six runs in the first two innings of the next night's game and the Otters fall, 7-2.

On to Chillicothe, where Evansville loses, 7-5 and 4-2.

"Everything is spotlighted when you don't win," Brian Harrison says. "Guys complain like with the bus and they look at errors with more of an evil eye."

Harrison is hitting .340, but he hasn't let that lessen his anxiety about being cut.

"I walk on eggshells every day. I'm still caught up in being a rookie. I feel like a peon. In college, I was probably the most sure-of-himself guy on the team. Now I'm just the opposite."

Shwam doesn't like Harrison at third because he boots too many balls. He plays a little at first, but most of his starts come as designated hitter.

"Early on, they didn't feel the need to replace me when I was hurt because we were winning. Now, geez, we're two games below .500. Why should the man DH a rookie when he can DH a veteran?"

Harrison says he thought his time had come a couple days ago when he got an early-morning call from Carmichael.

"I went in there like it was death. Turns out there were a couple of pitchers he wanted to look at and he needed somebody to catch."

I ask if he's accepted Shwam's managerial style.

"Yes, but it's killing me. I want to know where I stand. Am I here or am I gone? Tell me something."

JUNE 27

Chris Cosbey's elbow is hurt.

"If I try to throw, it feels like somebody is beating it with a hammer. The only thing I can do with the bat that doesn't hurt is bunt."

This doesn't come as a surprise. Cosbey has a long history of bone spurs and arthritis. He had season-ending surgery in 1999 when he was with Modesto. Doctors have said he'll have to be cut on at least every other year if he keeps playing. His left arm is bent as if someone took the stuffing out of it.

"I love the game too much to go out there when I can't help the team. Selfishness enters in, too. If I'm not at my top level, I have no chance of getting picked up."

He comes to the park early on this off day for treatment. He says Shwam will give him a few days to see if rest will help.

"If I can't play soon, I'm gone. I know that. He can't have a center fielder with a busted wing."

I enjoy watching so many of these guys play.

Harrison, because it makes him so happy.

Mattingly, because he would block home plate against a truck.

Thomas, because of the way he slides into second.

Richter, for his preparation.

Miller, for his grace.

Coronado, for the way the ball jumps off his bat.

But most of all, Cosbey.

Beating out bunts. Stealing bases. Playing with a corkscrew for an arm. Those Munchkin hands and feet.

And the way he covers ground in the outfield.

One night, from our vantage point in the bullpen, we saw him come within an inch of making a back-to-the-plate catch Willie Mays would put in his book of dreams. With the fence only a few feet from his face and closing fast, Cosbey dove head-first and skidded onto the warning track. He retrieved the ball in an instant and held the runner to a double. Everybody in the bullpen bowed like they were in the presence of greatness.

Cosbey ignored them and popped his fist angrily into his mitt.

"The little bastard thinks he should have caught it," Brandon Mattingly said.

Eric Cooper observed that Cosbey looks like a papoose with cleats.

"If that dude is just average size, he's playing Double-A, don't you think?"

"Guaran-fucking-tee it," Mattingly said.

Hudson is also injured. Says the muscle in his left shoulder is killing him. Says he told Shwam not to waste his spot in the order on somebody who can barely grip the bat.

Scott Suraci is released.

His replacement is John Raffo, recently cut from the South

Atlantic League. Big guy. Lefty. Will play some outfield, but mostly first base. Likes to play pinball. Fondles his bat between innings. Says it needs love.

Todd Brown is activated to play second base. The guy Shwam started the season with couldn't hit. The guy he brought in quit the team after eight games. Told the skip he wasn't having fun.

"Fun. That's a new one," Shwam says. "Career called off on account of fun."

JUNE 28

Evansville comes back to win the second game, 6-2, against Cook County, but the series opener is typical of the season.

Down 2-0, Harrison draws a walk. Cosbey is inserted as a pinch runner and promptly steals second. Raffo plates him with a single.

Last inning. Leadoff man Brown walks. Chris Adams can't get a sacrifice bunt down, not even on the third try. Thomas' single is wasted and the Otters fall, 2-1.

JUNE 29

Coronado is back in the lineup. His shoulder is better, but his digestive tract isn't. He throws up four times, twice during the game. After being picked off third, he heads straight for the clubhouse to blow chunks.

The game goes back and forth and there is much scurrying around in the bullpen. Blaylock gets up. Then Richter. Then Steele. Then Blaylock again.

Josh Hudson is in charge of the radio, which, unbelievably, is working this night.

The catcher says something to the effect of, hey, Britt, what say you make up your mind whom you want up, dude.

Carmichael says something to the effect of, hey, numb nuts, it's a close game and don't give me any shit, and you'll get your fat ass up when I say so.

Hudson takes immediate umbrage.

He has perhaps the most trim ass on the team. Britt is the one with the fat ass, maybe even fatter than Shwam's.

"Mix in a salad," he hollers into the radio. "You know, that green stuff on the other side of the mashed potatoes."

Carmichael isn't polite with his response.

Hudson responds by throwing the receiver onto the field.

It's a Radio Shack timeout.

The game stops while Hudson walks around the fence into the right-field power alley to pick up the equipment. In the dugout, Shwam's glare is smoldering.

The Otters win, 9-7, in 12 innings.

Mark Thomas comes up to me after the game.

"Need a title for your book?" he asks.

Absolutely.

Thomas shows me what passed for the warmup ball the last time the outfielders took their positions. The thing feels like it has spent the last two weeks in a wading pool.

"Big bold type," he suggests. "'Can't Find A Dry Ball'."

JULY 30

Cosbey is back in center field. I watch him throw between innings. He just flips the ball as he would to an eight-year-old. At the plate, he winces every time he swings.

"Chris is hurt," says Coronado, his best friend. "His arm is just hanging. He can barely lob the ball to the infield."

The dugout is subdued. All eyes are on Cosbey. It's like a death watch.

Seventh inning. Runner on second. Base hit up the middle. Possible play at the plate. Cosbey fields, cocks, throws.

And grabs his elbow in agony.

Shwam runs to the outfield. He gets down on a knee and consoles Cosbey, who is fighting back tears, not from the pain as much as what the pain means. Becka arrives and walks back to the dugout holding the injured arm as if it's on a serving tray.

Cosbey sits at the end of the dugout and puts a towel over his face.

Thomas is the first player to arrive.

"Is it over?" he asks.

Cosbey looks up long enough to nod.

"Fuck," Thomas says. "It's not fucking fair."

The others make their way to the little bundle under the towel.

Nobody knows what to say to someone whose arm is turned sideways.

They tousle his cap, gently squeeze his good elbow and walk away. It's like folks paying respects at a funeral home.

"Can I have some Tylenol?" Cosbey asks politely.

Becka doles out the pills.

"Four's the limit," she says.

"Like at a nightclub, huh?" Cosbey says, smiling.

I think back to what Shwam said a few days ago in his office about the pressure he's under to release guys who can't help the team. Cosbey has missed five games already. He doesn't lead the league in any category except smallest pants size. No way Shwam keeps him.

Mattingly and Raffo hit home runs and the Otters best Cook County, 5-2. It's their third win in a row.

The bus pulls in front of Bosse Field. The team leaves for Springfield in a few minutes to be ready for tomorrow afternoon's game.

It has taken some doing, but Cosbey has managed to get his shirt on. He puts his bats in the equipment bag. He is making the road trip.

"Dan hasn't said anything. Maybe he wants me to pinch-run. Maybe the baseball gods aren't through with me."

Shwam is still in his office. It takes him longer to get dressed. Must accessorize around the knee brace.

Cosbey, I point out, can't throw a dart, much less a baseball.

"Not gonna cut him. If I had 24 guys like Chris Cosbey, we'd be in first by five games."

No offense, skip, but even you could hit a one-hopper to him in center and leg out a double.

"Not gonna cut him."

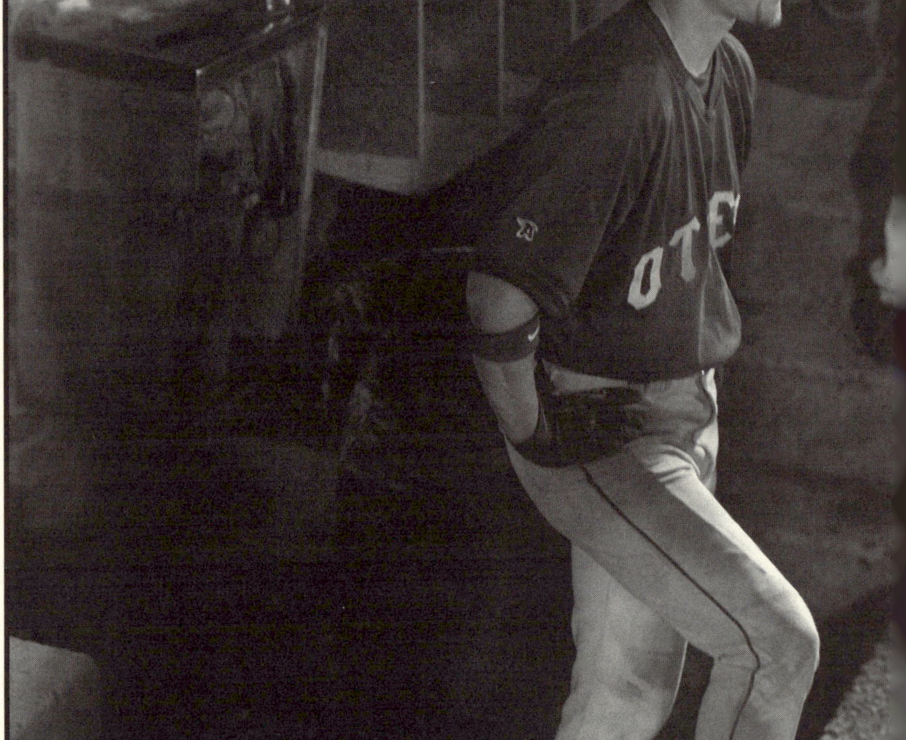

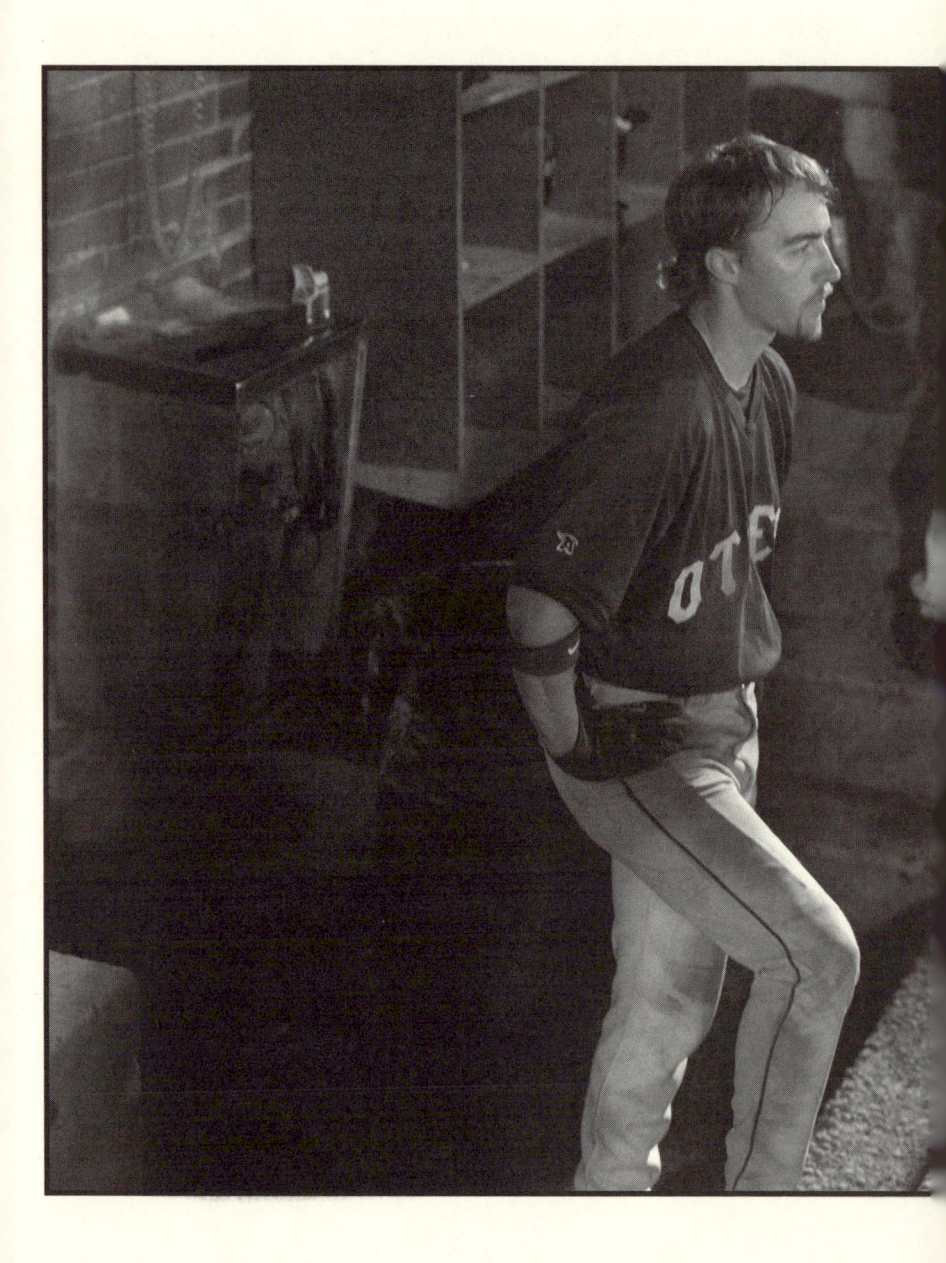

5

The Far Eastern Connection, Cos and the Kite Man

WHO ARE THESE two folks scrubbing down the locker room?
Why, it's Bill and Phyllis Bussing.
"The job needs to be done," Bussing explains. "Our family name is all over this venture and we take a lot of pride in that. The players play. The owners clean. Nothing wrong with that."

JULY 1

On the bus, the team watches the football movie "Remember The Titans," on the several screens.

Everybody swears Raffo is crying at the end, although he denies it. Shwam goes to the back of the bus and embraces Raffo and says, hey, this is the 21st century. It's OK for guys to show their emotions.

The players howl with laughter.

It takes the bussie almost an hour to find the hotel. When the team finally arrives and checks in, several players find nonfunctioning toilets and air-conditioning units that don't work. Some are reassigned to second, even third rooms before everything is as it should be.

Evansville goes down easy, 7-1.

"Zero energy," Harrison says disgustedly. "We came in here like a high school team."

JULY 2

Miller pitches into the ninth of a 3-3 game. Enter Richter.

Walk. Stolen base. Hit. Otters lose.

"I committed a sin against baseball," Richter says. "Britt comes out to talk to me and I tell him the next guy up isn't any good. The baseball gods (groan) will slap you in the head. He hits a shot off a slider and we're beat."

JULY 3

Evansville gives it up in the late innings again, this time on a game-deciding home run off Stelzner. He doesn't immediately leave the field, which almost causes a fight.

"The guy hits a bomb and I'm pissed," he says. "Dude takes his time circling the bases. I'm watching every step. They mouth off at me. I give it right back. I'm a competitor. It's not over until it's over. Maybe he'll miss third. Maybe he'll miss home. I'll tell the ump and we can still win. I wasn't trying to antagonize anybody."

Shwam doesn't see it that way. He tells Carmichael to get Stelzner the fuck in the dugout where he belongs.

JULY 4

Steele is released.

Hudson is released.

I ask Shwam if the flinging of the radio entered into his decision.

"He wasn't hitting, but that didn't help any."

Cosbey remains with the team. He got a cortisone shot and Miller has him doing a series of movements and stretches.

By way of bulletin board information, Cosbey wrote "Cos Is Still Here" on a strip of adhesive tape and stuck it above his locker.

Williams is still not hitting. He mopes around the dugout, rarely speaking.

Evansville has signed Eduardo Figueroa, an outfielder/first baseman.

Native of Puerto Rico. Graduated from the University of Tennessee with a degree in sports management. Drafted in the 29th round. Speaks impeccable English. Married to Emily, an Australian. Says they're a Rand McNally couple. Says he has absolutely no idea what he will do with his life when he isn't playing baseball any more.

Played two years in the Midwest League. Was released in spring training by the Kansas City Royals. Elegant. Gentle. If the baseball gods really exist, they'll quarantine him from Thomas.

Growing up, Figueroa played with Alex Cora of the Los Angeles Dodgers. He was on the same winter ball team with Jose Valentin of the Chicago White Sox.

"Sometimes I'd have two hits in a game and Jose wouldn't get any. I'd go home feeling on top of the world. But the major leaguers always come back strong the next day. If Valentin and the other guys have a bad at-bat, they stay calm. They know they'll be successful next time. The rest of us aren't so sure. That's the difference."

Is it true what I hear about Latin fans?

"In Puerto Rico, the fans yell and heckle like crazy. The arguments aren't just with the players. You have entire families being insulted. It's different with the umps, too. They just don't stand there and take the abuse like they do in the States. Sometimes the umps punch better than the players. There's a heavy police presence, too. Rifles. Machine guns. It's a little dangerous, but very exciting. You get used to it."

Cooper leaves word that his grandfather is ill and he's flying out to be with him in California.

Harrison is convinced he's going to be cut.

"How many guys we got now at first base?" he asks.

He counts on his fingers.

"Raffo, Thomas, Me, Figgy. Shit, let's have a big party over there. Get a DJ."

No walkie-talkies for the bullpen tonight.

"Those damn batteries have cost me thirty bucks already," Carmichael says before the game. "Got to be a better way."

There is. At least, it's another way.

Shane Smuin gets a start and pitches five solid innings, leaving with an 8-3 lead.

Carmichael hollers for his runner.

"Go tell Love to get loose."

Mike Butler is off to the right-field fence where he hollers the news. With no toga to worry about falling off, he arrives in record time.

Message received and confirmed.

Who needs fiber optics?

JULY 5

Brandon Mattingly is 8-for-16 since Hudson got hurt.

Mattingly was also thrown out of a game for threatening to beat the shit out of a pitcher who chuckled after hitting Figueroa in the chest.

"I've rededicated myself to baseball," Mattingly announces.

He admits his morale was low the first four weeks of the season.

"I let some things bother me that I shouldn't have. I'm a second-year guy and there are rookies making more than me. Shwam said there wasn't any more money available. It was take it or leave it. I took it, but I was pissed. It wasn't bad enough that Hudson had my position. He had my money, too.

"When I wasn't playing, I was hollering and screaming in the dugout like always, but my mind was somewhere else. I was thinking, shit, what about the rest of my life? I want to be a cop."

Whoa. Brandon Mattingly on the police force. This takes time to sink in. This is Mattingly, the flex-your-nuts guy, the slurp-up-a-loogie-for-$100 guy. You mean we're going to give this person a badge and a six-shooter?

"Maybe not. The guys on the team say I'll flunk the psychological exam."

Let's put aside the image of being pulled over and seeing you waltz out of a squad car. Back to baseball. What got your mind right?

"Getting it through my head that something I've loved since a little kid might be almost over."

His face hardens.

"And I wanted to put it in Shwam's face for not making me the starter in the first place. Every hit I get from now on, I'm going to look over at him and say, 'That's for you, buddy.'"

Mattingly gets two knocks, including a double, as Fry gets a complete-game 6-1 victory over River City.

Darren Oliver is a starting pitcher with the Texas Rangers. Don Blaylock tells the bullpen about working on Oliver's Jeep Wrangler.

"The shop foreman gives me the work ticket. I see 'Darren Oliver' and I say, 'Oh, God.' The vehicle wouldn't start, so me and some guys pushed it in the garage. We ran tests, but it was just a dead battery and shit.

"When Darren came to the service area, I ran in and told him a little about myself and asked for some pitching tips. We had a brief conversation and then I went to get his Jeep. But it wouldn't start. Dumb me left the dome light on. I was nervous as could be.

"Why did there have to be a screw-up on this man's ride? I

grabbed the jumper box and did my thing while he waited outside with his golf clubs. I never charged a battery so fast in my life."

JULY 6

Jewell Williams is released.

"The guy was a chemistry problem from Day One. I knew that," Shwam says. "He was a crap shoot. I was hoping we could ride his potential. But he quit hitting and lost his drive for the game. This is probably all she wrote for him. He had a chance to dominate this league and he didn't get the job done."

Williams was not popular in the clubhouse.

"He bragged to some guys he was our team's franchise player and that meant he got more money," one player told me. "We knew that was bullshit. Then there was the story about getting signed for a suitcase full of cash. They don't do that sleazy stuff any more."

The skip denies a rumor he is about to sign two Cuban defectors off the team that beat the Baltimore Orioles in a spring exhibition game.

But the team has added two players from another hemisphere, Yuji Nerei and Tomohiro Honda, from Japan.

Nerei, 26, appeared in several games last season for Ottawa, the Expos' Triple-A team. Quit high school 10 years ago to come to a tryout in San Diego. Was one of the first Japanese position players to make it to Triple-A. Played with three teams in the Montreal organization before being signed by St. Paul in the Northern League. Didn't hit enough home runs to suit them so he came to Evansville. It became a package deal because St. Paul refused to keep Honda—who speaks no English—without a translator.

If Nerei doesn't catch on with an affiliated team, the outfielder/designated hitter will go back to Japan and place his name in that country's professional draft. Says he could earn $100,000 if signed.

Nerei is a law student in Japan. Has reasonably good command of English, but slang is something else again.

Harrison watches him hit line drive after line drive in batting practice.

"Hey, don't big-league me, dude," he calls out, grinning.

Nerei runs over to pump his hand, thinking a miracle has happened and Harrison has been signed by a major league team.

Honda is trying to learn the language. He has a child's reader, "What You Do On Sundays" in his equipment bag, along with a workbook of practice sentences.

Bottom of the ninth. Game tied at 4. Chris Adams walks to lead off the inning. Cosbey enters the game to pinch-run.

There's no farting, spitting or grab-assing in the Otters' dugout. Everybody stands on the edge of the railing. They know this could be the last time this kid plays ball.

Raffo sacrifices him to second.

River City doesn't need a Ouija board to know what's next. One, two, three pickoff plays. Cosbey is filthy, but unfazed.

"He's going," Mattingly predicts. "I'd bet my dick."

Cosbey is halfway to third before the ball leaves the mound. The catcher throws, but only to prove he's on the job. The runner is already brushing himself off.

Three pitches later, the ball gets under the catcher's glove and rolls toward the backstop. The catcher scurries after it, actually believing all is not lost.

Cosbey doesn't bother to slide. He motors right into his teammates' arms.

Watching the Otters whoop it up, the value of games and why we play them becomes clear.

It may take hundreds of innings. Hundreds of halves. Hundreds of periods.

But it will happen. A game will result in the perfect outcome. The right team will win. The right person will be the hero.

"If this is it," Cosbey says, slapping backs and shaking hands, "thanks."

JULY 8

Top of the first against Gateway.

Jeremy Coronado hits a grounder to first. The pitcher covers the bag. The throw isn't a good one. Runner and fielder collide.

The Otters go on to score eight runs in the inning. The pitcher tells his higher-ups that Coronado elbowed him and that's why he couldn't get anybody out.

Their bench buys the story. The next time Coronado comes up, he is called a host of bad names. One coach tells Coronado he is a dead man.

"I kept waiting to get hit the whole game," Coronado says. "They threw at me three times, but it didn't happen. I was nothing for six, but I hit two balls hard. I'm proud of that."

The Otters go crazy on the basepaths, scoring 16 runs in the first three innings. Figueroa has four rips and six RBI. Nerei, Mattingly, Keith Law and Chris Adams each have three hits.

Late in the 20-4 rout, the home plate umpire gets hit with a foul ball and has to leave the game.

Guess who replaces him?

The team mascot, of course.

He takes off his costume, puts on a blue shirt, grabs an indicator, hops the fence and joins the game.

Talk about your multi-faceted guy.

Brand says he wishes he had talked with guys who played for Shwam before coming back to Evansville.

"We're not affiliated. We need communication. It's that simple."

A bad-hop grounder hits Law in the grille. Blood flows everywhere. Not wanting to soil his uniform, he walks off the field like someone who can't straighten his back.

Becka takes him to the emergency room. He isn't treated for almost four hours. When a nurse finally comes and tells him to open wide, Law spits blood and the woman gets mad at him for making a mess.

The shortstop finally gets his 14 stitches. His swollen lip looks a Goodyear radial.

Trainer and player don't get back to the motel until 3 A.M. Becka is exasperated.

"I used to think I was lucky to have a job that doesn't involve french fries. Now I'm not so sure."

Stelzner is told he is on the brink of being let go.

"It made me mad, but a different kind of mad. I said, 'If you want to release me, then release me.' I mean, don't hold it over my head. How is trying to scare me going to help?"

JULY 9

Coronado knew it wasn't over. He knew Gateway hadn't forgotten the night before. He just didn't think it would happen with the Otters up by two runs.

Eighth inning. Carmichael overhears the plotting to nail the second batter. He informs the plate umpire who says, "Yeah, well, what of it?"

The first pitch hits Coronado in the back.

"The catcher gets in my face and tells me to start something," Coronado says. "The next thing I know, he pushes me and my helmet goes flying. I don't want to fight. I'm innocent."

Both benches come out and Thomas is ejected for inciting to riot.

"Utter bullshit," Shwam says. "The poor kid gets hit. He tosses his bat down and starts to first. The catcher pops him with a forearm to the back of the head. Jeremy says, 'God will get you for this.' They told me he cussed. Jeremy wouldn't cuss if he was on fire.

"That's what gets me so frustrated with this league. The umpire should have thrown out the pitcher and manager right away. That would have made the catcher think twice about what he did. But the ump didn't establish control and the catcher assaulted a guy. That's low class, very low class."

Coronado gets a measure of revenge. He swipes second and third, giving him four stolen bases for the game.

JULY 10-12

All-star break.
>The Otters are 20-19.
>Thomas isn't hitting .300.
>Harrison is.
>Fry is 4-0.
>Brand is 1-2, but with a 1.27 ERA.
>Coronado is afraid of dogs bigger than his shoe.

Nobody keeps a pitching chart like Tom Miller. Some hurlers blow the job off, figuring who gives a crap if it was a slider or a changeup. But Miller fills in the little boxes like a high-priced accountant. If the enemy hitter lines the ball to right center, Miller draws the dotted lines to that spot on the form as carefully as a battleship navigator. He is repeatedly erasing and starting over. It's like he is turning this in to Picasso, not Shwam.

>Butler is hitting .115.
>Love is 1-4 in six starts.
>Steele was 0-4 with 14 runs allowed in 16 innings.
>Williams hit .207 with 37 strikeouts in 111 at-bats.
>Becka says the farting is harder to get used to than the spitting.
>Law sometimes wears a dress during pre-game warmups.
>Stelzner worries about his mother, who has breast cancer

and refuses chemotherapy because three of her friends have died from it. He has given up three home runs in 11 innings.

Cosbey can throw 90 feet without pain. The strip of adhesive tape is still above his locker. Somebody has added a couple of exclamation marks.

Coronado is still on a mission from God, to Shwam's dismay.

"We've talked. I said, 'Shit, son, don't proselytize. It makes guys uncomfortable.' I told him if he wants to do that stuff away from the ballpark, that's fine. Hell, I'm a devout Catholic. Go to church every chance I get. But when we're in the dugout, we need to be thinking about winning, not about who's going to the devil."

Brand and Coronado are the team's representatives at the all-star game at Cook County. Brand pitches a shutout inning in the 4-1 loss to the Eastern Division. Coronado gets one of only two hits.

"I thought it was great to be selected, but the event itself turned out to be a letdown," Brand says. "Was there somebody from Major League Baseball to talk to us? No. Was there a killer buffet? No. What I'll remember the most were the line dancers who got booed off the field.

"I saw eight scouts with radar guns, but they all left before the game was over. The only thing good to come out of it was there was this big bucket of baseballs that nobody was paying any attention to. Some real pearls. I made off with a couple dozen and nobody suspected a thing."

JULY 13

Trouble with Eric Cooper.

The hurler's story: Before leaving to be with his ill grandfather, he talked with Shwam and was assured he would keep his spot in the starting rotation. When he returned, that wasn't the case. Honked beyond belief, Cooper does everything but announce on the PA that he was screwed over.

The skip's version: "When Cooper left, all I got was a message that there was a family emergency. He was gone for a week. When he came back, I told him to give me three days and then I'd activate him. That wasn't soon enough for him and he started yapping about me not being a man of my word."

A lot of guys like Cooper. Always has something to say.

Mattingly's exhortation of "Let's get some shit on the board" notwithstanding, the Otters are lifeless.

Tom Miller gives up four home runs and is taken out with the team down, 7-6.

He is almost in tears when he gets to the dugout.

"I'm too frigging old for this. One laser shot after another. It's like they knew what was coming."

Harrison does his part to make Miller feel better.

"Shit, dude, if you were pitching against me, you'd be up 6-0."

Love consoles him.

"It just happens sometimes, Tom," he says gently. "One game last year, I got lit up for 15 runs."

Stelzner hits two batters in the eighth. Shwam is ejected for arguing balls and strikes.

Raffo fouls off an 0-1 pitch on which Coronado had second base stolen and then casually kicks dirt off his cleats.

"Asshole doesn't even know what he did wrong," Mattingly says.

Honda goes in to pitch. A Dubois runner gets to second. Mattingly can't change the signs because he can't communicate with his pitcher. The runner reads the catcher's fingers and flashes signals to the hitter.

Nolan Fry sees it all and isn't happy that the opposition is taking advantage of the fact Mattingly didn't take Japanese as an elective.

"That No. 12 wants to play bush, I'll play bush. I'll drill his ass."

The Otters fall, 10-8.

Coronado says he knows what this book's title should be. A solemn team picture and then...

"The Just Shall Live In Faith."

JULY 14

During a game, players often talk about things completely unrelated to baseball.

So far this season, the following subjects have been bandied about:

- 'N Sync.
- The food value of Cheese Whiz.
- How Todd Brown is afraid something will happen to Becka if she goes off alone during road trips and insists someone always go with her.
- The pros and cons of popping stimulants before going to the mound.
- The chemical makeup of piss.
- A drinking game in which losing a round calls for the loser to be slapped with a shower thong.
- The notion Tom Miller should officially change his name to Professor.
- Whether you'd rather die or have a coat hanger caught in your balls.

I asked Brand if such seeming disinterest in the matter at hand would bother him if he was on the mound.

"Only if the people having the conversation are on my bad side. Three hours is a long time. You can't think baseball every minute."

JULY 15

Thomas, while eating a cheeseburger before getting dressed for pregame workout: "I'm amazed at what people don't know about baseball. We come to the park three hours before the first pitch, even before that if we're on the list for early work. We're hitting, throwing, fielding, running, all that shit. They think we roll in a few minutes ahead of the national anthem, pop the ball in our gloves a few times and then hit the field. What a joke."

Carmichael, running his hand through his hair as he's seen Shwam do: "I realize I could be better with communication. Maybe be more of a friend to the players than a coach. I know I wasn't Dan's first choice. We talked forever before he gave me the go-ahead."

I tell him some members of the bullpen say there is confusion out there.

"They've told me about that," Carmichael says. "Sometimes the game can spin on a dime. The other night, I had Blaylock up and Dan wanted to stick with the starter. I want them to tell me if they've got concerns. It'll make me better at my job."

Adams and Coronado get three hits apiece to lead the Otters to a 7-5 win over Dubois. Richter, who has taken over the closer's role from Stelzner, pitches a scoreless ninth for his third save.

Best exchange of the season:

Raffo was hit in the bean the night before, so he is asked, "How's your skull?"

Raffo does a perfect impression of someone rendered nearly brain dead.

"You say you want mashed potatoes with that?"

JULY 16

Cooper is released.
 Law has his stitches removed and promptly pulls a hamstring.

JULY 17

I arrive at the dugout a few minutes before game time. As is my habit, I check the lineup card to see which position players aren't playing and will thus sit in folding chairs outside the dugout both to protest Shwam's decision and to acknowledge their unworthiness vis-a-vis the starters.
 Chris Cosbey is in left field.
 He tested his arm the day before. Two different Otters saw the demonstration and report Cosbey can't throw much better than a high schooler.
 "If he gets in the game, it's all right here," says one of the players, putting his hand over his heart.
 Cosbey sits by himself in the far corner of the dugout. Except for the maroon jersey, he could blend in with the cinder blocks. As is his way, there is no loud trumpeting about coming back when everybody thought he was gone.
 "The cortisone shot helped and I did everything the doctors told me," he says simply. "My arm isn't as strong as it should be, but I'm not feeling much pain."
 Cosbey looks out onto the field.
 "I just want to play. That's all."
 The Otters stink. Brad Love gives up seven runs and three wild pitches in five innings. Gateway bangs out 13 hits and takes advantage of four Evansville errors on its way to a 12-5 romp.
 Cosbey has a double and single in four trips. On defense, he doesn't have to make any strong throws and spends most of his time running down hits.

Tom Miller and I watch him put his gear in his bag after the game.

"I've seen humble before," Miller says, "but this is ridiculous."

JULY 18

Butler is released.

"He was definitely upset," says Chris Adams, who thought it prophetic that Butler was listening to "Love Hurts" by Nazareth when Shwam put out the call.

"But he knew it was coming. All he did in BP for the last couple of days was try to hit bombs. He feels like he didn't get enough at-bats to prove himself. Mike might have been the best glove man on the team. I think this is going to have an effect on morale."

Adams remembers the night Butler stole his truck.

"I was talking with some girls at a bar after a game and he thought I was going to leave with them. So he takes my keys and drives off. I didn't think too much about it at the time, but then closing time comes around and I don't have any wheels. I end up walking more than two hours to Mattingly's apartment. Next day, I call about my truck and Butler says, 'It's a lot more rested than you are, dude.'"

Adams says he's mostly pleased with his season so far.

"I've run us out of a couple of innings, but I know I'm contributing. Only a couple of times have I struck out on good pitches. I'm know I'm a little rough skills-wise—not polished, you could say—but I use that to make me the underdog, so I'll try harder."

How worried are you that you might have a bad 10 games and be gone, too?

"A few weeks ago, I was very jittery about it. Then I realized I belong here. Even if the Otters give up on me, other teams will pick me up. The coach at Gateway talked with me after a game. He said he likes the way I play and he'll hold a spot for me."

For good luck, he says, Mattingly has created a sort of baseball montage on the clubhouse floor. Bats, jockstraps, used dip, Power Bars, sweatshirts, shoelaces. Each item is arranged just so. To really cement the team's fate, he is considering pissing on his creation.

Mattingly is careful to make certain Coronado's bat doesn't touch anything.

"Don't want it to start preaching."

Shwam says there is too much "negative shit" going on.

"It comes from some of the guys who get released. Instead of going home, they come to the park every day and whine about what happened. It creates a poisonous environment. You can't ask them to stay away for the betterment of the team because they'll say fuck the team. They want the team to lose to prove what I'm doing is wrong. They even root against their buddies to try to make it come true.

"This never happened in the Northern League. That's because you've got one day to leave. The team pays your bill out of town, takes you to the airport and says bye-bye.

"I wish there was a rule like that here. These guys are moaning and groaning to their host families about how they don't have enough money to get home. The host families say, aw, geez, you poor things, and let them stay on for free.

"I mean, shit, what's so appealing about being unemployed in Evansville? Is it the opera or something else I don't know about?"

"What's funny is that some of them actually think they can talk all this crap and then turn around and ask me to help them get a job. I'll personally see to it that they're out of baseball."

Will you call a team meeting?

"I'll give it a few days to see if the light bulb goes on and they realize they'll never get signed from this league if they let what happens to somebody else affect their performance. We've got some smart guys. I'm hoping this isn't something I'll have to chew on them about."

JULY 19

More new players.

Infielder Gabriel Delgado and catcher Al Ready, both of whom came over in a trade with London, Ontario. And utilityman Rob Skinnon, who takes Butler's place.

Delgado, a switch-hitter, was born in Puerto Rico and played at Oklahoma City College. The young man is deadly serious.

Mattingly hits the ball maybe 10 feet.

"I could fucking punt it that far," he screams, throwing his helmet. "I'm no fucking good."

The catcher doesn't really mean that. There's a volcano under his crewcut which requires some kind of release, especially when his effort at the plate would not travel past the arc chalked off on a tee-ball field. It's either spout off or run his fist through the dugout wall and miss three weeks.

"Why don't you just quit?" Delgado says in searing broken English, his eyes staring straight through Mattingly. "Go to the clubhouse. Put on your shirt and pants."

Mattingly waits for the punchline, but there isn't one.

Just icy silence.

"Shit, dude," Mattingly says, standard baseball lingo when you get trumped.

Delgado, a first-year player, was glad to get out of Canada.

"I go on a 12-game hit streak and what happens? The manager puts me on the bench for three days. Then I play some games and get my average over .300 and I sit again. When I got traded, the manager said he was sorry for jerking me around. I didn't take his apology. You do good, you should play. That's it. No talk."

Ready, who lives in London, was one of three catchers on the team and played infrequently. Hit 18 home runs for the University of Indianapolis, but didn't get drafted. Computer guy. Very tall for a catcher. Face has "Aw, shucks" all over it. Think Goofy in a chest protector.

Skinnon just graduated from the University of New Haven in Connecticut. Small at 5-7, 170 pounds. Hasn't picked up a ball in three weeks. Says Shwam probably heard about him from his college coach.

"I had hung up my spikes and was working at a landscaping business," says Skinnon, who looks like a semi-grown-up version of Beaver Cleaver. "It was crazy. I couldn't afford the $600 for a plane ticket, so I took the bus from New Haven to Evansville. Took 30 hours. No change of clothes. No brushing teeth. Just butt in seat the entire time. When I finally got here, they lost my luggage.

"I got to the ballpark with no glove, no bat, no nothing. My parents are on a cruise to Alaska. They have no idea where I am. I'll call when they come back and say, 'God, you guys won't believe this. I'm in the Midwest and they're paying me to play baseball.'"

Most of the Otters try to be cool about being on the team. Not this new hire.

"July 16th," Skinnon gushes. "My 23rd birthday. The day I signed my professional contract. I was actually jumping for joy."

River City gets an unearned run when first baseman Raffo throws away a potential double-play ball at second.

After the third out, he sits by himself in the dugout.

Mattingly gets in Raffo's face.

"Quit fucking pouting," he screams, spewing dip every which way. "You think your shit don't stink?"

The lecture takes hold. By the time the second hitter gets in the box, Raffo is standing on the top step with everybody else.

"I can't stand it when guys separate themselves from the team like that," Mattingly says later. "You can be a lone wolf in a zoo, but not in baseball."

Honda gives up two long fly-ball outs. Shwam tells Carmichael to talk to him. The pitching coach is more than willing, but confesses he knows less Japanese than Mattingly, if that's possible.

Shwam confers with the home plate umpire and then motions to Nerei.

"Go with Britt," the skip says. "Blue says it's OK. Be a translator. Tell him to keep ball down."

I watch my first international conference at the mound. Nerei really gets into the advice-giving bit, babbling incessantly and making sweeping motions with his hands.

"Yugi should have those little earphones," Richter observes. "Be like the United Nations."

Shortstop Delgado drops a pop fly in the eighth inning and River City breaks open a close game to win, 5-1.

On the bus, Shwam addresses the multitude.

"Don't give up on this season. There are 38 games left. Remember what I said back in camp. You can prove people wrong, or you can prove them right. Don't let somebody take the game away from you. We're all in this together."

Back at the hotel, Stelzner says it was one of the skip's best speeches.

"The man was positive for once. He put himself in the same boat with us. We sink or swim. He sinks or swims."

But the carping soon returns.

"Delgado drops the ball and costs us the game," Stelzner goes on. "Shwam should have done something after the game to pick him up—put his hand on the kid's shoulder or something. We're not machines out there."

The reliever notes that only 12 guys are left from the opening night roster.

"It's like he thinks we're a bunch of dogs. Get rid of one you don't like and bring another one in. We've had a good team all along. We just haven't been given the chance to gel."

Miller talks about hanging it up if he has another bad outing.

"If you go, I go," Brand says.

JULY 20

In the hotel lobby, Skinnon is making entries in a notebook. Assuming he's chronicling his career as an Otter, I ask to have a look.

It's anything but the diary of a reserve infielder.

He has penned page after page of mash notes to his beloved Erika.

I give it back. Gee, Rob, this is personal, more personal than your cup.

"We love each other," he says, beaming. "I'd show it to the world."

He writes about how pretty she is and how much he likes to fly kites and how she is the woman he has been dreaming about all his life and how he's a mama's boy at heart and how, when he holds her in his arms, the world is a big, bouncing balloon.

"If she was in town right now, we'd be out hiking somewhere. Hand in hand. Up and down the hills. Then she'd drop me off at the ballpark and I'd get three knocks. Perfect end to a perfect day."

Shwam says too many of his guys need time off.

"They busted their asses to make the team and then they thought they had it made. They started easing up. They're sleeping until noon. They're not lifting. It's real simple. They can stay in shape by their own decision or I can do it by leaving them on the bench."

He tells me too many players look at him as a deity.

"It's like they say, 'Shit, Dan went to the water fountain and it went in the right side of his mouth. Is that some kind of sign?'

"They need to learn. Don't ask me how you're doing. Do it for yourself on the field."

Big night for Yugi Nerei. Three hits, including a majestic home run over the right-field fence.

"There's more where that came from," the skip chirps. "He's gonna knock the shit out of this league."

Rob Skinnon is in the on-deck circle.

I know the plan. He's on the team for a week until Law heals. Then it's back to Connecticut.

But what if he gets a bunch of rips? Shwam would have to keep him, right?

The kid walks to the plate.

Come on, son. Do it for the kite-flyers of this great nation.

Line drive right at the shortstop. He couldn't have hit it any harder.

Eighth inning.

OK, Rob. Last chance of the night. Erika wants you to do it. I want you to do it.

He slams the first pitch to the right side. The second baseman leaps like he's on a trampoline and hauls it in. No knocks in five trips.

There is a total lack of justice in baseball.

Nolan Fry goes all the way in the 12-5 win.

Thomas slips on the wet grass going after a long fly. Shwam makes it a point to ask between innings if he's all right. The players stop what they're doing and take note. The skip has been doing this sort of thing more and more. It's like he really does give a shit.

On the bus back to the hotel, Harrison tells Thomas, who went 3-for-5, that he is living his life through him.

Nerei climbs up the steps.

Mattingly bows, puts both hands on his two feet of extra belt and swings it wildly.

"Ah, so. Great samurai."

I take a seat beside Skinnon.

He grins.

"Almost did it, didn't I?"

You're right about that, I reply. Twice you had me out of my seat. So close. An inch either way."

"They're gonna release me, aren't they?"

I tell him I'm not privy to front-office decisions but, yeah, you're probably history when the team gets back home.

"Nobody can take this away from me," he says.

Anyone who would try should be forced to ride Greyhound to upper Manitoba.

JULY 21

Get-away day.

Brand explains.

"You wake up earlier than you'd like and get everything packed. Stay in your room until the hotel throws you out and then you take your stuff to one of the two rooms the team pays an extra day's lodging for. You get 10 or more guys in there playing video games, watching TV or trying to read until it's time to go to the field.. There's absolutely no space, but the worst part is everybody has to take a shit after coming back from lunch and the room stinks something awful. After the game, the bus leaves for the next city and you don't have to go back to the hotel. The get-away thing saves money, but the whole afternoon feels like you're crammed in a packing crate."

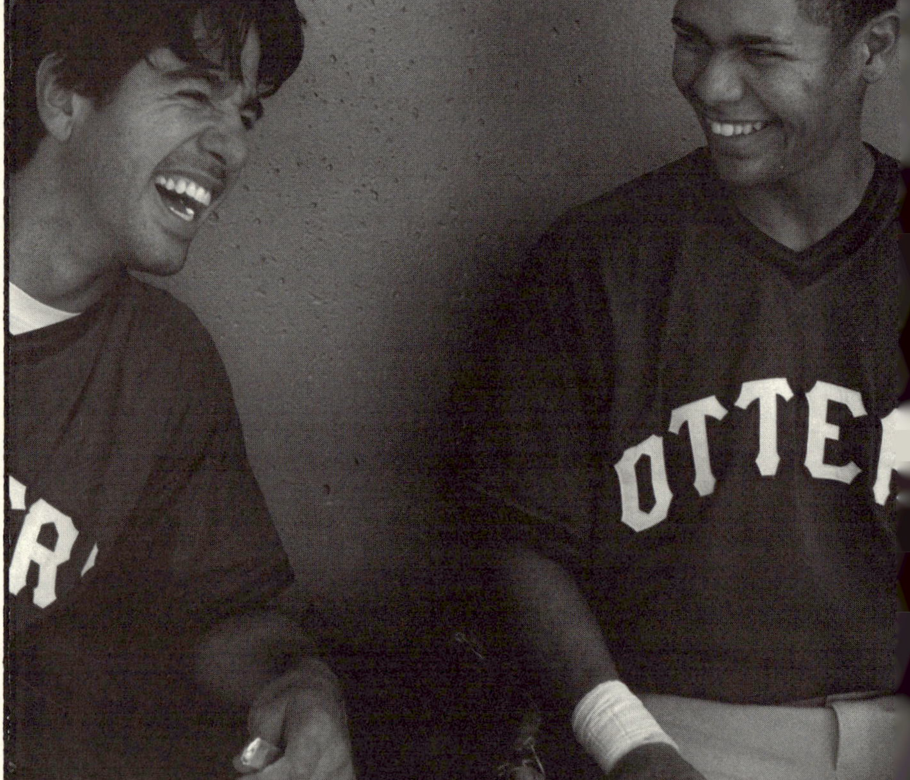

6

The Dawn Patrol

JULY 22

Very, very early morning.

The bus arrives at the appointed hotel in suburban Chicago. Ahhhhh, yes. Take a load off, grab some shut-eye, prepare for the series with Cook County.

But no.

The clerk says no reservations, no rooms. Sorry.

It's after 7 A.M. before they finally find an establishment that can accommodate 24 ass-dragging ballplayers.

Naturally, it's oppressively hot and humid and several rooms have less than stellar air-conditioning units.

Only four hours until time to go to the park.

Shwam is pissed.

"This is a good way to steal the first game of the road trip. Make up some bullshit about how there aren't any rooms and the visiting team ends up having to drive to Timbuktu. They sleep-walk through nine innings and the home team gets the W."

Gateway's starting pitcher, Chris Moore, has an asthma attack in the dugout after the sixth inning. He almost dies before the paramedics arrive.

Not long after play is resumed, John Raffo fouls a ball off his leg. He shakes it off. He strides toward the next offering and goes down like a victim of sniper fire. His leg flops around like a snake that has been hit by an ax.

His tibia is broken.

Raffo is carted off the field and loaded into an ambulance. Becka goes with him. Shwam calls Raffo's parents in Florida and tells them to pick him up.

"The guy took it well," Richter says. "I was impressed."

The Otters aren't very impressive and lose, 9-3.

JULY 23

Rainout.

Fry: "There will be some beer-drinking tonight."

Coronado: "Drunkards will not inherit the kingdom of God."

JULY 24

The Otters drop the first game, 5-1, but win the nightcap, 2-1, in 11 innings.

Nerei drives in the winning run. He's batting .430.

On the way back to Evansville, the bus stops at the hospital to pick up Becka, who is with Raffo.

"You wish it didn't have to be like this," she says. "It was cold, real cold. The team moves on and he stays. Raffo looked so all alone. I know he's a big guy and all that, but I felt sorry for him."

JULY 26

Before the doubleheader with London, a baseball is passed down for everyone in the dugout to autograph. Happens all the time. A kid buys the souvenir at the gift shop and players fill in the space around the picture of Evan the Otter.

But this is a practice ball. Dirty. Scuffed. Seams frayed.

Some of the players refuse to attach their names to the ratty thing.

Not Tom Miller.

"It's not the quality of the ball," he explains, Aristotle-like. "It's the quality of those who sign it."

Fry is ahead, 1-0, in the late innings. He walks a batter and Carmichael tells Mattingly to go to the mound.

The local TV camera guys have long since shot their game footage and gone back to the station. Following a trend that has continued all season, ESPN and the other national networks have elected not to cover the Otters game. The only satellite truck outside the ballpark belongs to the cable repairman.

There are maybe 1,200 people in the stands, the usual Bosse Field crowd in the absence of a reduced-price ticket promotion. None, to my knowledge, have listening devices.

Certainly, Johnstown's dugout isn't paying attention to the conversation on the hill. There's a break in the action, for God's sake. Time to fart, belch, spit and goose somebody.

Yet Mattingly and Fry put their gloves over their mouths to hide their words the same way they see the major leaguers do. They chat through the webbing like spies. Mattingly goes back to his position confident that his instructions went completely undetected on the world's radar screens.

The score stands. It's Fry's seventh win without a loss.

"Last year, I looked into the stands every night I pitched to see if there were any scouts," he says. "I tried to be cool about it. Catch a peek while a foul ball is going out of play. Three or four real high ones and you can check out the whole park. I'd get frustrated if I didn't see somebody. Not this season. Whatever happens is whatever happens."

In the second game, the Otters go up 6-0 on a three-run homer by Figueroa and a bases-clearing double by Delgado. Shane Smuin cruises, until the sixth. Law makes an error on a force play and then Smuin gives up a walk on a close 3-2 pitch. Visibly upset that he got squeezed, Smuin stomps around on the mound, glares at the umpire and pounds the ball into his glove. He walks in a run and the next guy hits a grand slam. Game tied. Stelzner comes in.

Miller gives Smuin a few minutes to cool off.

"Want to talk about it?" he says gently, holding the chart.

Smuin nods.

"Look at your pitch selection," Miller says, pointing to the little boxes on the piece of paper. "You were going with your slider too much. It was nasty, but you weren't throwing it for strikes. You had good gas on your fastball. That's what you should have been bringing up there."

Al Ready gets his first hit as an Otter. Knocks by Cosbey and Coronado and a pair of force outs and Evansville goes up by two.

Richter holds the lead for the save.

With the doubleheader win, the Otters climb to 28-27, four games behind division-leading Dubois County.

Rick Skinnon is released. He had two hits in 19 trips.

Bill Bussing and his laptop are in attendance. He hasn't missed a home game yet.

"Watch a play on the field. Call up a stock. I'm a two-way guy."

JULY 27

Mark Thomas hits a hard grounder up the middle. The shortstop lunges to knock the ball down and falls to his knees. He quickly rights himself, but his throw sails wide of first. Thomas is safe by two steps.

Desperate to get to .300, desperate to get out of here, Thomas looks at the scoreboard. Hit or error? A two-point swing in his all-important batting average is riding on how the play is ruled.

There's no immediate word from the press box. Maybe the official scorer is deliberating. Or maybe he's trying to do something about the huge wedgie he's gotten from the long game.

Then the news is flashed.

"E."

Thomas winces more noticeably than if he had been hit by a pitch.

He starts muttering. A constant stream.

Big bouncer to third. Thomas is forced at second. He goes in like the Special Forces, but can't beat the rap.

He runs back to the dugout, lips in high gear.

"What would it fucking hurt to give me a hit?" the right fielder screams. "He's up there scratching his ass and my goddamn career is on the line."

Thomas steps to the right corner of the dugout where his cap and glove are always neatly placed for the return trip to the outfield.

"Ten times this season this has goddamn happened. The moron says, 'Fuck, that should be a hit, but wait a minute. It's Thomas. Let's make it an error.'"

Honda goes all the way in the 7-2 win.

There's grousing in the dugout about how the skip almost never makes a move during a game involving position players. If you don't start, you don't play. No defensive substitutions. No pinch-hitting.

"It's hard to stay focused," says Harrison, whose time has been cut even more with Nerei taking over the DH slot. "You sit on the bench and it's one inning after another. Figgy could die at first base and Shwam would send his corpse up to the plate in the bottom of the inning."

Richter to Stelzner: "Your brain is like a super-computer. Always processing information. Then you get that look in your eye."

Stelzner: "Really. What look?"

Richter: "Like you've got no personality whatsoever."

JULY 29

Cosbey goes deep—a 330-foot rainbow that barely clears the right-field fence.

Coming back to the dugout, he gets the knuckle salute from his teammates, another thing these Otters have borrowed from the big leagues.

I ask if he's been invited to the home run derby.

"Yeah," he says, smiling. "Yeah, to the one in Williamsport (Pa., the site of the Little League World Series)."

The Otters lead, 6-0, but Richmond puts up eight runs in the seventh off Brand and Stelzner and wins, 9-6.

JULY 30

It's getting to be a habit.

Cosbey hits another home run.

He takes his seat in the manner of the shy little boy who solves a math problem at the blackboard and hurries back before anybody notices him.

Hey, there's going to be a little spotlight here, OK? Can't be avoided. You were almost shipped home. Now you're back in the lineup and hitting bombs.

"There's no pain in my arm and I can drive through the ball better. This is the first time this year I've felt really strong."

Is that all you've got to say?

"I'm very fortunate. A lot of people have worked hard so I can play."

Coronado comes by.

"Don't feel bad. He doesn't talk about it with me and we room together. He does this for the competition. It could be here. It could be Double-A. It could be sandlot. Cos doesn't care. He just wants the opportunity to test himself."

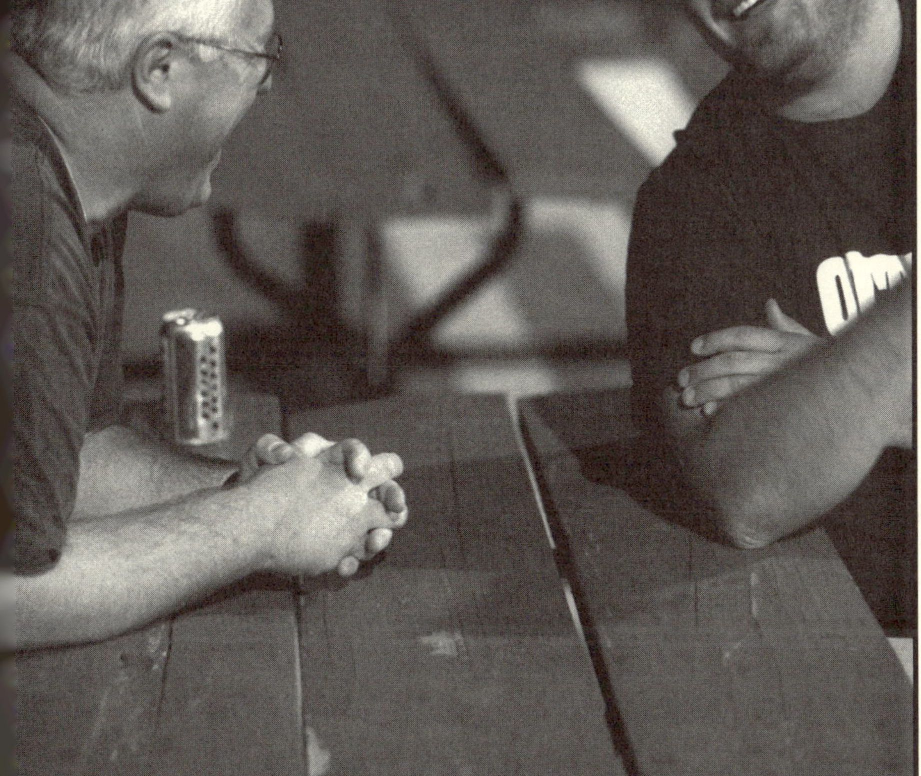

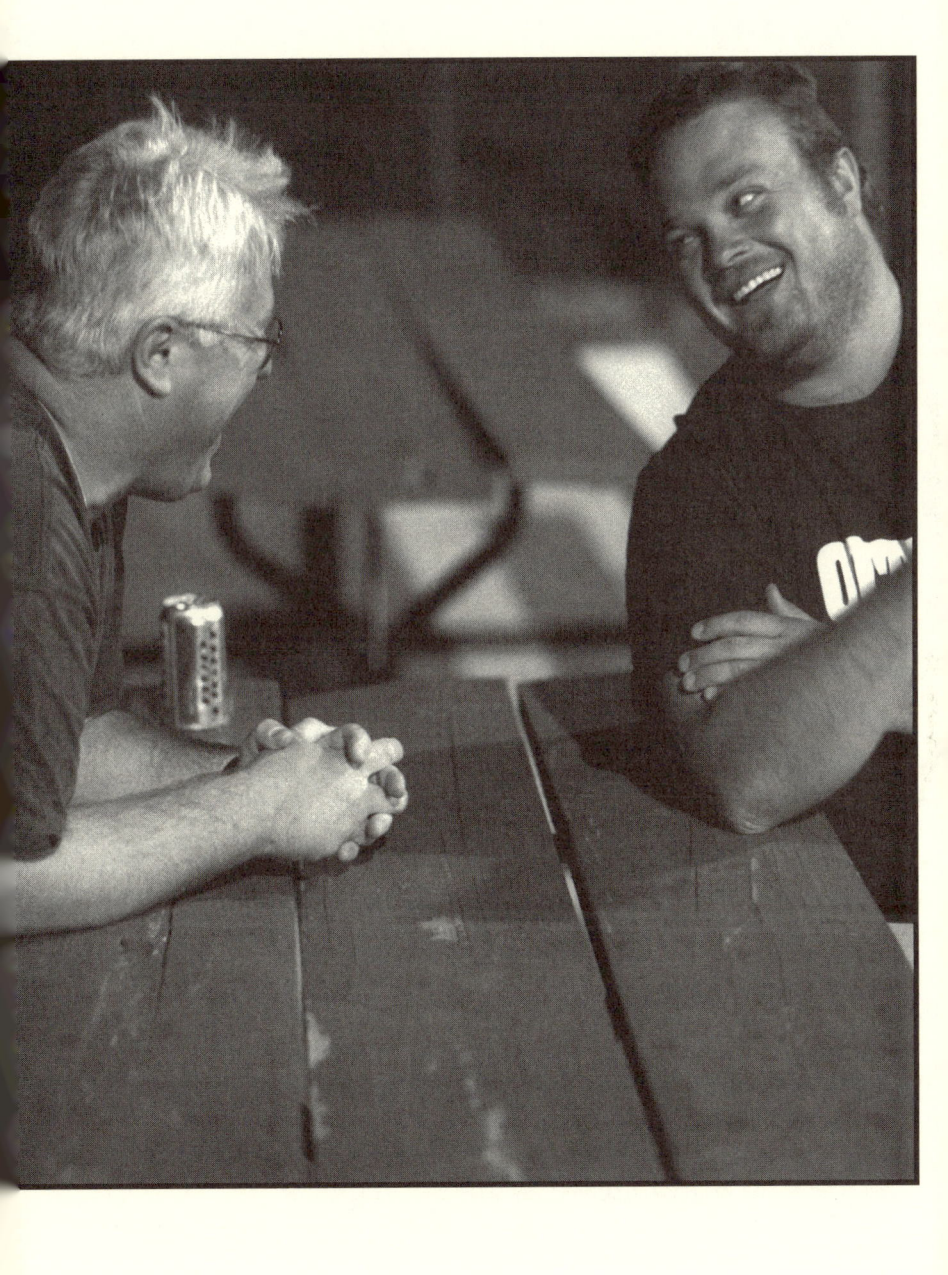

The Otters are down, 5-2.

Coronado misplays a fly ball in center. Figueroa is picked off second. Fry messes up a pickoff attempt.

Miller enters the game in relief and strikes out five in two innings.

Law makes a beautiful play on a slow roller to end a Richmond threat.

"Keith is the only one I can get to go shopping with me," Becka says, by way of observation. "He has really good fashion sense. The stuff he buys really goes together."

Nerei raises his bat perpendicular to the ground and stares down the pitcher.

"Let the hungry warrior feast," Miller says, looking on.

Two-run blast. Evansville rallies to win, 8-5.

Coronado's .383 average leads the league.

Cosbey has 24 steals and 10 bunt hits.

Richter has given up only two earned runs in 18 innings.

Raffo ends his season hitting .250 in 30 games.

Figueroa is batting .262, but has eight doubles and 13 RBI.

Thomas is up to .280.

Fry leads the staff with three complete games.

Smuin is 5-2 and the only starter with more strikeouts than innings pitched.

Adams, Mattingly and Harrison are around .300.

Stelzner is 1-2 with four saves, but he has walked 14 batters in 19 innings.

As an Otter, Ready only has the one hit in 11 at-bats. He has struck out six times.

Delgado has been on the team less than two weeks and already has 14 rips.

Coronado has been picked off five times. His teammates believe he was distracted by talking with God.

Richter wishes more pitchers would pay attention to the charts.

"The hitters' tendencies are right there on paper to see. It just takes a few minutes and it could be the difference between getting an important out or not."

Steele, Williams, Hudson and the others have left town.

Figueroa may be slower than Harrison. He runs like he's carrying a piano.

Becka takes dip on a dare, but not chew.

The skip is starting to throw some BP.

Carmichael believes Smuin has the best chance of the pitchers to move up.

"He has got the best fastball on the team and he's a competitor. The guy is laid-back everywhere else, but he's a mean SOB between the lines. The ump took a pitch away from him the other night and he nailed the blue in the thigh."

Honda is usually by himself if he is not with Nerei.

Harrison says he should learn some Japanese as a kindness to the young pitcher.

"But I'm a lazy piece of shit."

AUGUST 1

Evansville has an off day to make the trip to London, Ontario.

Well-rested and happy to be staying in a hotel that's downtown and within walking distance of restaurants, the Otters pound out a 8-5 victory. It's their eighth win in the last 11 games.

Coronado and Delgado have three hits apiece. Harrison gets a start at first because Figueroa's back stiffened up on the bus ride and socks a home run. Smuin has another strong outing, striking out seven in six innings.

Blaylock gets a rare chance to pitch and serves up four runs in the ninth. Richter has to come in to get the last two outs.

Shwam isn't happy with Adams' run production. Todd Brown is activated to play third base.

Coronado has found a way to make Mattingly stop cussing. "I hug him. Let him know he's loved. Shuts him right up."

AUGUST 2

Carmichael says he is hearing fewer complaints from the bullpen.

"One thing is that I'm talking to them more. Lift them up when they get down on themselves.

"And a lot of the negativity is gone out there. Back in training camp, guys were happy to get one of the 11 pitching slots. If they couldn't start, they said they were glad to go to the pen. 'Hell, yeah, be happy to.' Then they sat out there a few games and all that happy shit changed. They bitched and bitched about not getting the ball. Those guys aren't with us any more. Now everybody out there knows his role. It's a helluva lot quieter."

Evansville goes down, 7-2. Four errors lead to four unearned runs.

AUGUST 3

The worst road trip, Shwam says, the absolute worst.

If the bussie was a player, Mattingly fumes, he would be released.

It was so bad, Richter says, that "we were all delusional."

"It's the middle of the night and we're going to Kalamazoo," Shwam says. "I'm tired. The kids are tired. But, shit, we're supposed to be tired. I look over and the bussie is nodding off. It's his job to not be tired. His head jerks back up, so I'm thinking maybe we're OK. Then he starts to go to sleep again. That goddamn sure wakes me up. I don't take my eyes off the steering wheel the rest of the way.

"We get to town and I ask the bussie if knows where he's going. He says of course he does. Then he starts making all these left turns. One after another. Players counted six. Shit, I don't know. All I know is my neck was doing a lot of bending.

"It's like the bussie says, 'Shit, let's just wing it. Maybe we'll get there and maybe we won't.' More than an hour passes and we finally get to the campus of Western Michigan University. The bussie thinks we're supposed to stay in the dorm. We go to two different buildings and nobody knows jackshit about the Evansville Otters. Bussie grabs a map from this college kid and says, 'Yeah, well, maybe we're supposed to go to a hotel somewhere.'

"He reads that map up one side and down the other. I'm thinking, shit, we're cooking with gas now. Five minutes later he's lost again.

"Another hour goes by. Every road we go on is under construction. When he got up to 10 miles per hour, it was time for a celebration.

"Finally, we get to the hotel. The kids get their keys and we get all the equipment bags out of the bus. By this time, I'm more dead than alive. But at least I've got a room, right? Guess what? Somebody's in the bed. It was so bad it was funny. I said, 'Shit, guy, want some company?'"

Shwam says no road trip the entire season has gone smoothly.

Drivers get lost finding the hotel. Drivers get lost finding the field and the team is late for BP. The bus smells like piss. The home team changes the host hotel and doesn't bother to inform Otters management. There's confusion about what time the team is supposed to check in. Evansville arrives at 2 A.M. only to find the reservations call for 2 P.M.

"I call our front office in the middle of the night and tell them we're getting screwed at the hotel. The guy says 'Deal with it'' and goes back to sleep. I'll tell you what. I've done almost as much dealing with it as I have managing a ballclub. I know they took the cheapest bid on the bus company, but Jesus Christ, you save a few bucks and we all get heart attacks because we're afraid the man is gonna fall asleep on us.

"It wears on you. A five-hour bus ride becomes seven hours. The kids get on the bussie. The bussie gets on the kids. Your morale starts to go. You think, shit, if our organization cares about us, they sure have a funny way of showing it.

"My mistake has been not getting more directly involved with this end of it. I've been assuming that the paperwork has been done and the arrangements made. Maybe I need to be travel coordinator, too."

Kalamazoo wins, 5-2. The Otters get only three hits.

AUGUST 4

Another loss to the worst team in the league, this time by 7-3.

"If Coronado, Cosbey or Delgado don't get on, we're screwed," Shwam says. "Somebody besides Yugi in the middle of the order has to pick us up. It's like the other guys are hitting with swizzle sticks."

AUGUST 5

Laundry woes continue, this time in Richmond, Ind.

The home team is responsible for taking care of the visiting team's dirty uniforms.

Sometimes it doesn't happen.

At Chillicothe, the job fell to Becka.

"I sucked it up," she says.

At Gateway, the detergent crew was less than expeditious with their duties. The last Otter wasn't outfitted until 15 minutes before the game.

In Richmond, nothing is happening uniforms-wise, so Carmichael grabs a handful and starts to go to the Laundromat.

The woman at the front desk takes pity on a pitching coach

carrying half his weight in smelly tops and bottoms.

"She tells me to leave them on the floor and she'll do it out of kindness," Carmichael says. "Lady didn't want any money, but I gave her some anyway. You couldn't let anybody do Mattingly's jersey for free."

The clean Otters fall, 12-4.

AUGUST 6

Evansville claims the final game of the road trip, 5-1. Smuin gets win No. 7 and strikes out 12. Todd Brown hits his first home run.

Shwam calls a meeting.

"We joked about the bus. We joked about the laundry. I told them not to let these bad things be a reason to end your career. I said it'll be different next year. Maybe we'll make it like college and I'll drive the bus. Or be like Legion ball and go in a caravan. My car is the first in line and the kids follow. Dress in the back seat like in the Little League. We'll be the Dirty Two Dozen."

Richter says it was a good give-and-take.

"I was glad to see that Dan was mad. All this crazy stuff might help us bond as a team. It makes you realize you don't have the God-given right to play."

Figueroa puts it in perspective.

"We're in the Frontier League. The cash flow isn't there. We can't demand the best of anything. We don't have a parent team like the Brewers to pay the bills. You don't bitch about it. You just laugh."

AUGUST 7

As is usually the case, two boxes of baseballs are in the locker room for the players to sign.

Yugi Nerei picks up a pen and wades in.

Some Otters might be willing to forgive and forget the road trip, but not Mark Thomas.

He runs his forefinger across his throat in slashing fashion.

"Bus trip horse shit. No sign balls," he says.

Nerei doesn't understand.

"They fuck us over," Thomas explains. "We ride pissy bus. He no find hotel. We get even. We no sign balls."

Richter's family has come all the way from South Dakota to watch him play.

B.J. says his dad manages a 2,800-acre farm with 300 head of cattle.

"This is a major sacrifice for him to be here. It shows how much he cares."

Chris Adams isn't happy about being benched. He shows it by taking his folding chair to the side of the dugout a full 30 minutes before the game and plopping down on it.

"I've had no explanation whatsoever from Shwam," he says. "I was in the lineup and, all of a sudden, I'm not. I don't do much pre-game any more. I don't stretch. I don't lift. It's bullshit. There is no way I'll ever play for that man again."

Harrison brings his chair to Adams' side.

"It's a kick in the teeth for me to watch Todd to play third," Harrison says. "I don't hope he does bad, but I want to play. The way things are going, I'll be lucky to get a dozen at-bats the rest of the season. What do I do? Quit and go home? I have to try to make the best of it, but that doesn't mean I'm not hurting inside."

There are some stay-at-homes who believe the play at this level is unworthy of their $5. They miss a good show.

Second baseman Delgado cuts off a grounder in short right, whirls and throws the runner out at first.

Honda knocks down a line drive, crawls to retrieve the ball behind the mound and flips to second for the force.

Thomas chases a foul ball from deep right and catches it as

he falls over the bullpen fence.

Runners on first and third. The trail guy takes off. Mattingly fakes a throw to second base and guns to third. The lead runner is trapped off the base. The Otters get out of the inning.

Cosbey is at first after a single. Delgado lines a two-hopper up the middle. Cosbey stops at second but accelerates when the center fielder spends an extra millisecond getting the ball out of his glove. He does a pop-up slide into third, arriving well ahead of the tag.

"The key word is consistency," Shwam says. "On any one at-bat, Nolan Fry could get Chipper Jones out. Our kid might wear the line drive in the grille, but the out goes up on the board.

"Jeremy Coronado goes up against Greg Maddux. Maybe he doesn't get too much movement on a pitch and Jeremy gets a base knock the other way.

"But could our guys do it every day? No, and that's why they're at this level. It doesn't mean they're not any good.

"Some of our hitters might actually do better in Single-A or even Double-A because the ball is around the plate more. The pitchers have better stuff, true, but it's not going to be over your head or behind your back like it sometimes is here.

"The biggest adjustment would be the speed of the pitches. I don't know how many of our kids could catch up with a 94-mile-per-hour fastball. It gets in the catcher's mitt and they turn around and say, 'Oh, shit, somebody get the number of that train?'"

Honda loses, 1-0, to Dubois County. At 32-32, Evansville is in fourth place in the West, five games behind Dubois with 20 to play.

AUGUST 8

I ask Nerei how baseball is different in Japan.

"If a rookie pitcher hits a veteran with a pitch and does not tip his cap, he will pay a fine.

"The time before the game is a lot harder. You have a full three-hour workout and then the first batter goes out. It's like the military. Americans don't like it very much."

What about the great American pastime, spitting?

He shakes his head.

"If you did that, it would mean you don't like yourself."

Louie Carmona joins the team as backup middle infielder. Quiet. Criminal justice major. Wants to be a probation officer. Had two exams left to take at Southwest Texas State when he got the call from Shwam. He estimates playing the last three weeks of the season will net him $240. It cost $241 to fly to Evansville.

Nerei hits his seventh home run. While running the bases, one of the opposing players hollers something to him in mock Japanese. Rounding third, Nerei looks into the dugout to see who heckled him.

Bad form, I'm told from the Otters' encampment.

"You absolutely do not make eye contact with the other team when you hit a bomb," Mattingly explains. "You put your head down and get the trot over with as fast as possible. Looking in the dugout is showing them up. You don't want to build any bad bridges."

Hmm. Only Mattingly could bring civil engineering into baseball behavioral theory.

But I do notice finger-pointing on the Dubois side of the field.

"Next time up he's gonna wear one," Mattingly predicts.

Meanwhile, the popcorn-eating bat boy is slow to retrieve Nerei's weapon.

"Do your job," Thomas says, snarling.

The Otters register 12 hits and take a 10-5 lead.

Coronado is hitless in four trips. It's a repeat of his performance of the night before. He stomps up the runway and emits a loud noise that sounds like, "Argghh," although the acoustics from that venerable chamber have been confounding listeners since before the Second World War.

Cliff Brand squeals, he's so excited.

"Jeremy cussed! Jeremy cussed! Called himself an asshole. Plain as day. Call off the prayer meeting."

Nerei comes up again in the eighth. The first pitch is three feet behind him.

Mattingly is stomping mad.

"Puss," he hollers at the mound. "If you're gonna hit him, then hit him. Don't fucking bullshit around."

Nerei looks to the bench in confusion. Let me get this straight, he seems to be thinking. My teammate is ragging on the pitcher because he *missed me* with the pitch.

But he gets a hit anyway.

Richter comes in to pitch the ninth. Dubois loads the bases on a hit, a walk and a hit batsman.

"Not tonight," Carmichael moans. "I couldn't stand the pain."

Easy grounder to Delgado. B.J. heads straight for his family members, who run to the edge of the field as if the Otters just won the World Series. They line up to embrace their pitching star. Flashbulbs pop all around.

Evansville may be a small stage, but it's a bright one.

B.J. tells the Richters he'll be with them in a few minutes, but for right now he has to get back to the guys.

The farting guys. The knuckle-salute guys. The guys who would wear a pitch for the common good, but not let you make off with a bag of their sunflower seeds.

B.J. enters their midst and doesn't come out any time soon.

He has two families tonight.

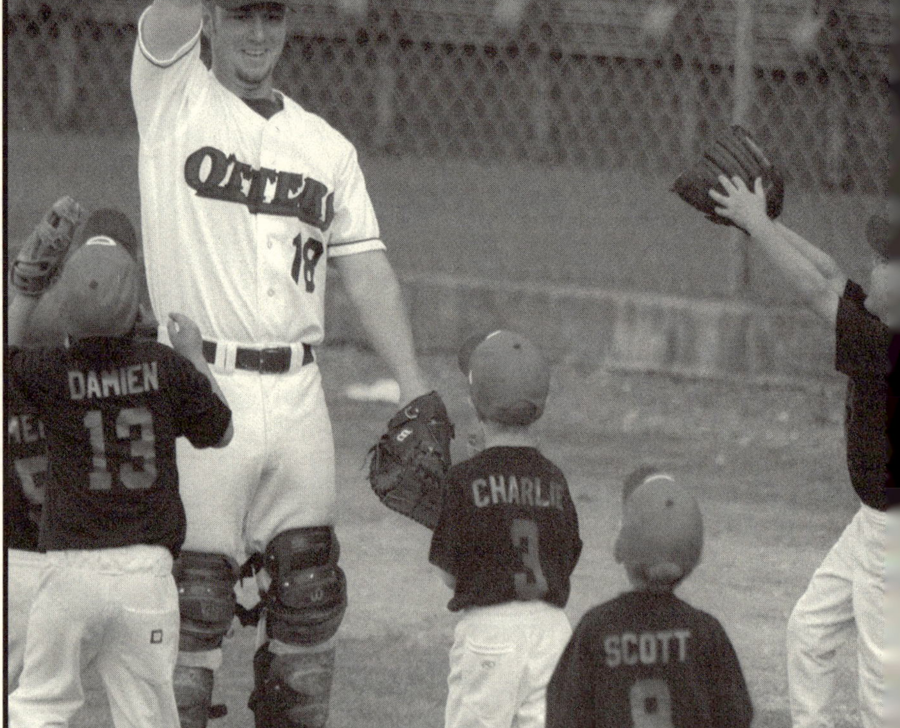

OTTERS
18
DAMIEN
13
CHARLIE
3
SCOTT
8

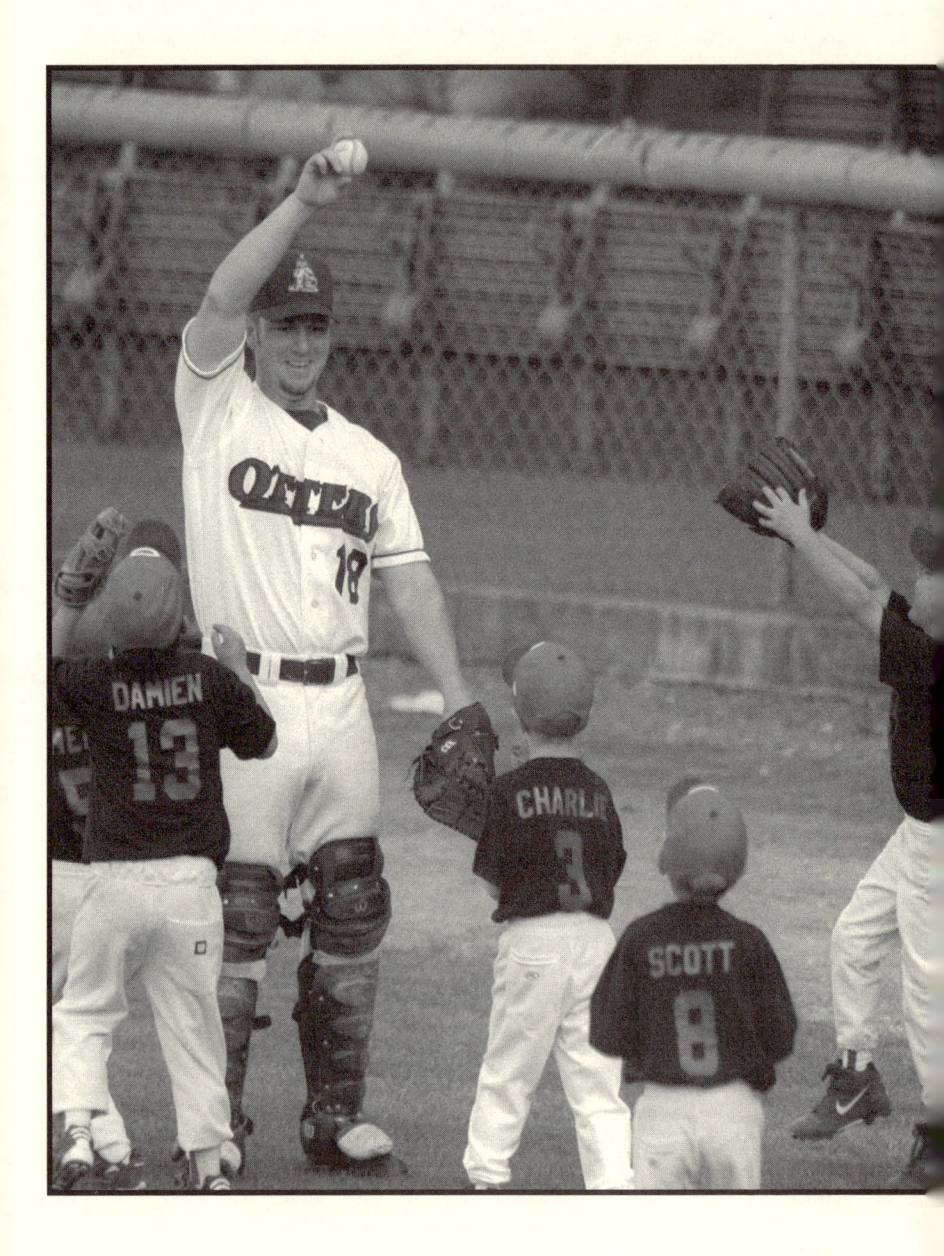

7

A Brotherhood, Just Like the Elks

AUGUST 10

Several players come up to the skip before the game and ask if he's all right.

"I got dehydrated the other night," Shwam explains. "It was a hot night and I was excited we won and bouncing around and everything. Then, all of a sudden, I had zip in my tank. I got light-headed and I know I didn't look so good. It was nice of them to check up on me. It shows what kind of kids they are."

Mattingly is in a frenzy. The first pitch is only minutes away and there's no Becka.

A little kid in the stands calls down to Smuin and asks if they can have a catch with his ball. The pitcher says maybe later, but for right now he has to play with people his own age.

A half-dozen Otters are talking with their host moms and dads along the fence up from the dugout. For those with 9-to-5 jobs, this is about the only time they can connect with their players. One man shows photos he took of a previous game. A woman hands out bags of fruit.

Becka appears.

"Fuck, dude," Mattingly calls out. "Where have you been? You know you've got to stretch me out."

Becka, more forcefully than she's been all season, "I was in the bathroom."

The Otters go up 3-0 on Springfield after an inning. The soft rain that was a welcome cooling agent turns into angry pellets. Nolan Fry retires the side in record time and hustles into the dugout. You know it's a bad storm. When Fry takes off his cap, his advice to himself is dripping down the bill.

Thomas almost fell in the muck going after a foul ball.

"The outfield is a fucking lake. I don't care if they goddamn release me. I'm not going back out there."

Fry has a different outlook, one he wisely shares in near-whisper.

"What's the name of that big weather system?" he asks.

"El Nino," Cosbey replies.

"No, El Nomo," Miller says, winking.

"Whatever," Fry says. "Let it take a little leak on the field and move on. My stuff is nasty tonight."

The grounds crew covers the field as the rain and lightning settle in. The floor of the dugout looks like an irrigation ditch.

"No game today," Love concludes, changing into flip-flops.

Coronado says his shoulder ached for almost a month after crashing into the fence at Gateway.

"It hurt to swing. It even hurt to run."

He smiles.

"I remember in college we used to get tired from playing four games a week and practicing two other days. The coach pushed us, so we'd be in shape to play in the pros. We complained then, but now I'm glad."

He says he'll take a month off after the season and then work on his footwork in preparation for next season.

"I've got a speed coach. Forty dollars a session. Just me and him."

Gee, Jeremy, you can barely afford lunch.

"My parents are paying. They've been with me every step of the way. In college, they didn't miss a game. When Pepperdine played in Hawaii, they hopped a plane."

A heavy-duty member of the grounds crew drops his load of sandbags. When he picks them up, his butt cheeks are on full display.

"Not professional," Cliff Brand says. "The team should buy him some better pants."

Ah, not professional. Another turn of phrase I hear almost every day.

It's "not professional" that the water cooler is drier than a desert.

It's "not professional" that there are never enough towels to go around.

It's "not professional" that the pen for signing balls doesn't work unless you beat the crap out of the point.

Becka says she has even heard the phrase when sitting with the players at restaurants.

"The mashed potatoes are 'not professional.' The service is 'not professional.' The tablecloth is 'not professional.' It's like the players have it rough as far as not making much money, and riding so many miles on the bus, and they're very sensitive to things they think don't measure up."

Love walks back from Shwam's end of the dugout.

"Checked with him to be sure, but I was right. This is it . . . No more cuts."

Harrison springs to attention.

"Don't bullshit me now."

Other Otters hear the news and come wading.

"League rule," Love says. "Teams have to set their post-season rosters by tonight. Can't add anybody. Can't subtract anybody. What you see is what you get."

A stick has been permanently wedged through Shwam's revolving door..

"Holy shit, I made it," Harrison exclaims. "I could hit into a quadruple play and not get released."

"Last men standing," Love says. "We're a brotherhood. Just like the Elks."

Keith Law says he's down to 163 pounds.

"I hit a brick wall two weeks ago. Couldn't hit. Couldn't throw. Couldn't nothing. Pitching in the Tigers' organization didn't prepare me at all for the grind of being a position player. Day after day, you slowly get worn down. I don't see how the guys in the bigs do it, February to October."

I point out that Barry Bonds *et al* don't ride 12 hours in a stinking bus driven by someone who may or may not know where he's going.

"Yeah, I know they fly everywhere and they have people to carry their bags and they sleep in nice hotels on monster beds," Law says. "But once they get to the ballpark, the routine is pretty much like ours—stretch, run, throw, hit, take grounders. Then the game starts and somebody takes you out at second, or you get hit by a pitch. We do 84 games and fall down exhausted at the finish line. The major leaguers go on like the Energizer Bunny."

The game is postponed. Evansville and Springfield will play a doubleheader tomorrow. The waterlogged fans head for the exits.

But who's this Ruthian figure strolling on the tarp?

Why, it's Brian Harrison in an oversized jersey pulled over a pillow. He's wearing giant glasses and has his hat turned backwards.

The baseball gods have spoken. There will be hijinks.

Yugi Nerei splashes to the mound. Holding an imaginary runner on first, he pretends to get his sign.

Harrison points with his bat to the left field fence. The gale almost knocks it out of his hand. He'll really have to flex his nuts on this one, sports fans.

Nerei winds up and plays air pitcher.

Harrison swings once, twice and goes down.

Much laughter.

The infielder has learned from all the comic geniuses. Timing is everything. Always build to a climax.

Another windup. Another pitch of night air.

This time the hit fairy connects. Far, far, far it flies. Harrison takes off around the bases like a young Curly Joe. He turns wide at first base—semi-slipping for maximum effect—and lumbers into second. But does our imaginary left fielder come up with it cleanly? No, he boots it. So, Harrison will attempt the impossible, otherwise known as a triple.

But why slide when you can belly-flop?

Harrison takes off where the shortstop would be standing if the low-pressure front had formed 400 miles to the south. He thunders into third faster than a bullet train. The water jumps out like a giant tsunami.

"Safe!" Todd Brown hollers. "The man is safe!"

It looked like the mermaid was in the perfect position to make the tag.

But that's baseball.

AUGUST 11

Bad omen. Brad Love is appointed to catch the ceremonial first pitch from a nine-year-old kid. It slips under Love's glove.

The Otters are up 4-0 after six innings as Fry only allows two hits. But Springfield rallies against Honda and the rest of the bullpen to win, 6-5. Mattingly makes the last out and obliterates the trash can.

In the second game, Brand leaves with a four-hitter and the lead. Richter can't hold it. He gets two quick outs, but a walk and a home run give the visitors a 4-3 victory.

There is a lot of beating and kicking. The walls of the runway. The clubhouse door. The bucket of practice baseballs.

Which brings us to cussing.

These are young males. Territorial males. This is my jockstrap. You can't have it. These are my sliding pads. Get your own.

It is necessary for them to mark their space. Raising their legs is a tiny bit too primitive, so they swear.

That's one reason. There's another.

They are members of a fraternity called baseball. Many go through rush. Few are tapped.

To join this outfit, you must stand in against a fastball that could send you to the emergency room. You must take the throw at third when maniac baserunners like Mark Thomas are bearing down on you. You must go all-out after a bloop hit over shortstop and hope to God you don't become one with your hard-charging left fielder in a teeth-loosening collision. Pitchers must hope that the muscle-bound cleanup hitter picks another night to send a line drive up the middle that reaches the mound so fast that a mongoose couldn't get out of the way.

Once you are part of this select group, you bond quickly with the others. Dipping and chewing helps, but cussing is quicker.

An F-bomb about such-and-such results in an, oh, yeah, me, too, F-bomb about so-and-so.

They're like a group of housewives getting to know each other over the backyard fence. Instead of giving each other marble cakes, they insult somebody's lineage.

Thomas and Mattingly cuss the most. No hesitation whatsoever. No final filter. Both, I'm convinced, would shake hands with the president next to his motorcade and say, "Hey, dude, nice fucking car."

Adams, Delgado and Harrison are a level below. These guys

pick their spots. The profanity must fit both the moment and their agitation level.

For example, Thomas and Mattingly could cuss while eating cookies with Grandma.

The other three would need provocation. Grandma burning the cookies, maybe. Or Grandma trying to big-league them by not serving them on the good china.

Ready has a decent vocabulary, but it's mostly to be sociable.

Stelzner can rip with the best of them, but only when he's pitching like crap.

Nolan Fry cusses the best among the starters, but that's not saying much. Brand saves it for walking off the field after the defense has just committed two errors and a passed ball behind him. Love is a no-no, as is Miller, who would assign himself five poles as punishment.

Blaylock will cuss to hold up his end of the conversation and that's about it.

Richter sometimes will throw a word or two into the mix, but only because he's writing his own script and wants to spice up the dialogue.

Ron Ryan, who looks like a Marine, usually sounds like one.

Shwam usually lays off the hard stuff, but he can say "shit" three times in the same subordinate clause.

The most effusive cusser is Britt Carmichael. Sometimes events on and around the pitching mound make him so livid that he forgets standard noun-verb usage.

Which brings us to my favorite outburst of the season.

"Son-of-a-bitching fuck-shit."

Shwam trudges into his office after the game.

"This was the season that could have been," he says. "We might still make a run at it, but we're too much of a win-one, lose-one team.

"I like our starters. The Midwest League is good affiliated baseball. Medium to high-level A-ball. You let us go up against one of their .500 teams and we'll split six games. Smuin, Fry and Brand will get some outs and we can throw in Miller and Honda.

"Despite what happened tonight, B.J. has been pretty damn good in the pen. But we can't get the game to him. Our middle relief has been bad all year. I have to go with the starters longer than I should. A guy can be dragging out there and I have to say, 'Son, can you go a little longer? Pretend like you're on a desert island and you know the rescue boat is coming, but it's not quite here yet.'"

Defense?

"Strong suit. Rabbits in the outfield. Cosbey, Coronado and Thomas can run the ball down with anybody. Not the greatest arms but, shit, you can't have everything. Delgado is a stud at second. You gotta play him every day or he'll pitch a bitch, but I'm OK with that. Mattingly is a bulldog behind the plate. Law is no Hercules at shortstop, but he's solid enough."

The skip sits back in the chair. The stuffing sags, but holds the load.

"Driving in runs is what we absolutely can't do. We get a couple of guys on base and it's like, shit, the moon is not right, can't let Evansville score. We're the enemy within. The other team doesn't have to mess us up. We do it to ourselves.

"Yugi got plunked in five straight games. The other teams aren't stupid. They know he's our only power threat. They're not gonna let him be the one who beats them. If they hit him, fine. Bring on the next guy."

Louie Carmona got his first hit as a pro in the first inning of the rainout. He called home that night. He admits being breathless.

"Dad asked if I saved the ball and I told him I was too busy rounding first. I said I'd get some other ball and we could just pretend."

AUGUST 12

Bottom of the first.

Cliff Brand pulls me aside.

"I've noticed something. Shwam always repeats what he hears in that high-pitched voice of his. Happens every inning . . . Let me show you."

Smuin shuts Springfield out in the second. As he does after every half-inning, Shwam marks on the lineup card which player made the last out. When he turns back around, the Otters are entering the dugout and preparing to hit.

"Listen."

Brand cups his hand around his mouth.

"C'mon now," he barks. "Gotta get some runs."

Brand winks at me.

Three seconds pass.

"C'mon now," Shwam exhorts. "Gotta get some runs."

Bottom of the third.

Otters come back to the bench.

Brand, just loud enough for the manager to hear: "Get on the board. Right here. Right now."

Shwam puts his pen in his pocket and claps his hand.

"Hey, guys, let's get on the board. Right now. C'mon, babe."

Brand is almost hysterical.

"Power of suggestion. Awesome, baby."

Once more, then I'll believe.

Bottom of the sixth. Evansville is up, 5-3.

Brand: "Smuin is busting his ass out there. Give him some support."

The skip takes off his cap and runs his hand through his hair.

"Smuin is busting his ass. C'mon, let's buck up."

Not perfect, but definitely impressive.

"I should take this on the road, dude," Brand says. "The Great Swami."

The Otters win, 9-3. Smuin and Love combine for 15 strikeouts. Mattingly drives in 4 runs.

There's only one more road trip—to Cook County and Springfield—before six games at home and the season-ending series at Dubois.

The skip tells his charges nothing will go wrong, that this will be the highlight reel of bus travel. Reservations have been checked and double-checked. We're Marco Polo no more, he says. There is a plan.

AUGUST 14-16

Evansville takes two out of three from Cook County.

Chris Moore, the pitcher who almost died from an asthma attack the last time the Otters were in town, goes six innings in his team's 4-3 win.

The next night, Delgado and Figueroa each get four hits in a 4-1 victory. Nerei is hit by two more pitches. Miller goes seven strong innings. Richter gets his eighth save.

Brand leads the way in the rubber game, pitching six shutout innings in the 2-0 victory. Al Ready doubles in the go-ahead run. Cosbey's two steals give him 31 for the year.

"Have a winning road trip," the skip says, "and the beer is on me."

AUGUST 17

Fry is lit up for eight runs in four innings, and gives up an uncharacteristic five walks as the Otters lose, 12-8, to Springfield.

Nerei is hit again, this time in the knee, and has to leave the game. Harrison replaces him at DH and pops a home run.

Coronado is batting .360, but he hits in the No. 9 slot this night.

"Sometimes he puts too much pressure on himself when he leads off, like he has to get on base ahead of Delgado every time up," Shwam explains. "This is like giving him a day off from that."

The skip believes in bunching his speed guys—Delgado, Coronado and Cosbey.

Not wanting to hit one of them third, Schwam has batted Cosbey last much of the time since the center fielder came back from the arm injury, despite Cosbey's on-base percentage of more than .400.

The bussie finds the hotel. He finds the field. His vehicle smells like Pine-Sol.

AUGUST 18

It's becoming familiar. Smuin pitches. Evansville wins. This time, it's 11-1.

Coronado scores four runs. Law hits his first bomb in more than a month. Figueroa and Delgado each get three hits. The Otters steal five bases, a season-high. Smuin again reaches double digits in strikeouts, with 10 in seven innings.

The bullpen has found a new game.

Bocce ball.

They fill a Mountain Dew bottle with sand and top it off with a sock. They place it on the other side of their bench and roll baseballs toward it. Closest to the target wins.

The entertainment after the game is a videotape of a melee that Delgado's former team, the London Werewolves, was involved in earlier in the year.

The second baseman rewinds the tape several times to show punches he claims to have landed.

"Floating like a bee," Delgado says.

Harrison doesn't buy it.

"Looks more like flying away like a butterfly."

The bussie finds the hotel. He finds the field. He buys sodas for his passengers. His coach is so clean the players are reluctant to use the toilet, believing it would be like pissing in a shrine.

AUGUST 19

Shwam is tossed for arguing balls and strikes.

Thomas is asked to leave after calling the plate umpire a cocksucker.

"The most incompetent umps we've had all year," Stelzner concludes.

"Not professional," Brand agrees.

Evansville builds an early 9-4 lead and hangs on for the 12-10 victory. With Nerei still sidelined, only one of their 14 hits is for extra bases. It's another three-knock night for Delgado and Figueroa. Richter gets the last four outs for his tenth save.

In the clubhouse after the game, Shwam starts to tell the players how proud he is of their 4-2 road trip.

Then Mattingly comes in stark naked and lies down on the floor under his feet.

The catcher rolls his eyes and half-crosses his legs.

"Aw, shit," a red-faced Shwam says, turning away.

The skip orders the bus stopped at the first convenience store. He purchases five 30-packs of beer.

The players go down the road more refreshed than a slow-pitch softball team.

Arriving at Bosse Field, the driver gets a standing ovation. A hat is passed up and down the aisle. It comes back full of tips.

Harrison: "Bussie went from Pony League to World Series."

Mattingly: "The guy was clutch. The only thing on the bus that smelled bad was us."

Richter: "There's a definite correlation between being getting treated better and winning."

Shwam: "I could take a nap without worrying about dying. It's like that commercial says. I got a new lease on life."

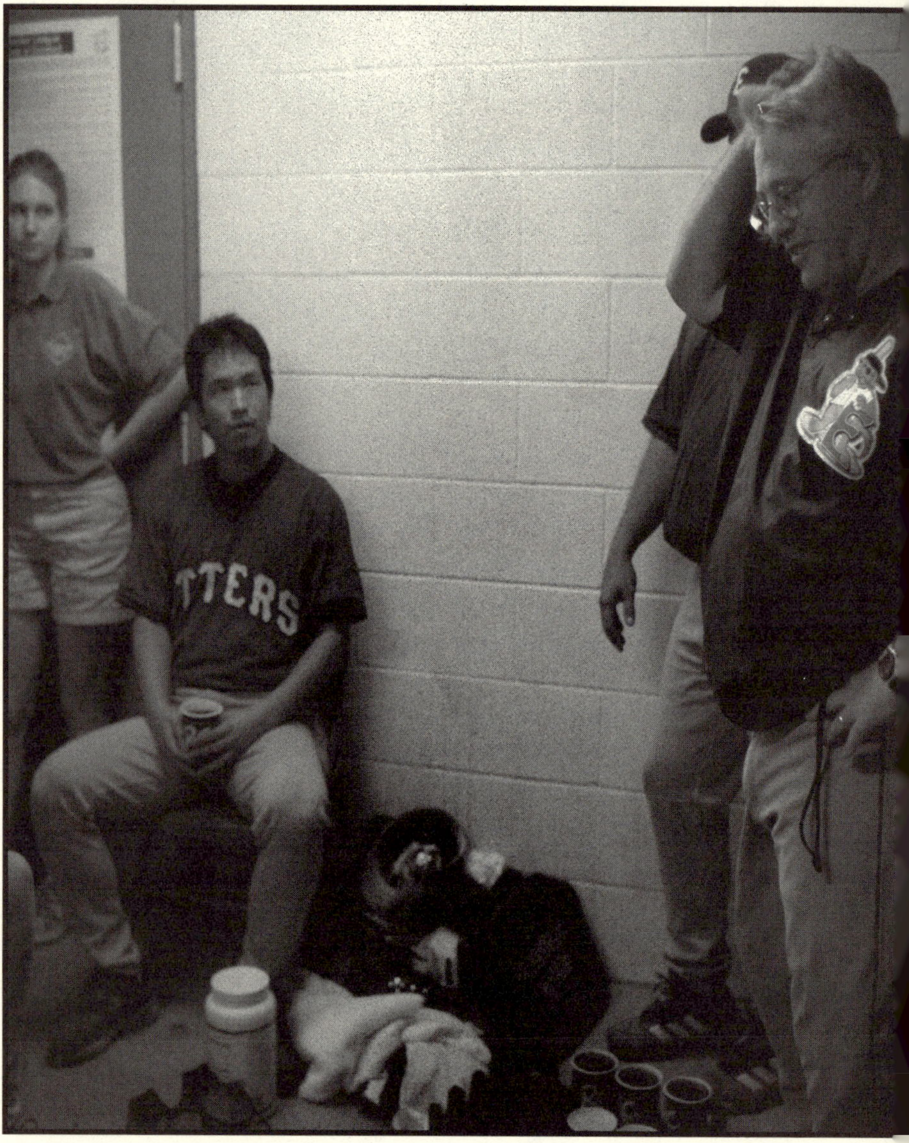
TTERS

8

Leaving Is Such Sorrow

AUGUST 20

Sore knee and all, Nerei belts a three-run homer to lead the Otters to a 5-2 win over Gateway. He has driven in 37 runs, averaging one for each game he has played.

"We're dangerous right now," Thomas says.

"I wouldn't want to have to play us," Law says.

"Anybody seen my glove? It's a good friend of mine," Richter asks.

Ron Ryan's son is in the dugout. He wants his father to see something.

"Daddy," he calls out.

Coronado looks up.

"How many other children do you have that we don't know about?" Stelzner asks Coronado.

Earlier in the year, Jeremy would either have ignored the remark because it came from heathen, or he would have started in with some serious soul-saving.

But, as he has done with his swing, the guy has made adjustments.

"Don't know," he replies. "The playground of God is a big place."

I ask Shwam about playing a set lineup and rarely making situational substitutions with position players.

"This isn't high school. Guys are on the bench for a reason. We don't have anybody there who can come up and give us a big hit."

Adams has continued going through the motions in pregame drills because he's honked about his lack of playing time. Yes, Shwam has noticed.

"Called him into the office the other day. Got out the box scores. Showed him the three hits in his last 50 at-bats. Showed him the five RBI since June 30. I told Chris he has to earn the right to play. I said, 'Shit, son, do you really believe I'll put you in a game if I see you not shagging balls and not taking BP seriously?'

"He thinks I have something against him. I said I don't function like that. I don't wake up and say, 'OK, I'm going to eat my cereal and then I'm going to fuck Adams today.'

"If Adams only got 40 at-bats, he can say he got yanked around. But he has more than 200. That's all the chances in the world.

"How you handle sitting on the bench is how you'll develop as a player. There's a whole lot less pouting in the Northern League. The attitude was, hey, I'll play in such a way that the SOB of a manager can't bench me. There's no 'woe-is-me' shit. There's no boo-hoo, I'm not playing, so I'll be a jerkoff. Nobody dogs it. They find out what they need to improve and that is what they work on.

"In that league, there would be veteran players who would come up to Adams and tell him to shut up and play. That hasn't happened here and I think that's one reason why we're only three games above .500.

"They forget this is a job. They forget I'm the CEO of this company. I don't have to give them ice cream and cake if I don't want to. How long would Adams last at IBM if he pouted when he didn't get the account?"

Shwam admits he's glad the trading deadline has passed.

"The phone doesn't ring. Nobody is going anywhere. I don't have to look over my shoulder. I don't have to listen to the owners throwing out names of shortstops, catchers and pitchers.

"I've gone through every emotion with these kids. I've defended them more than they'll ever know. I'm not a cold, calculating guy. I got caught up in what happened with Cosbey as much as the next person. It was a beautiful thing.

"I know managers who wouldn't just have released some of these guys for the shit they pulled. They would have damn near killed them. I'm not that rigid. I don't need to go to the dictionary to find compassion."

I suggest that perhaps one reason the season hasn't gone smoothly is that Carmichael and Brown are coaching for the first time, so more of the load has fallen on the head man.

"It took the Jaceys forever to commit to paying for coaches. Finally, they gave me $1,200 a month. I had two guys I talked to, but they wanted twice that. It's tough to find a guy who'll be your assistant when he's only making a little more than some of the players."

Some of his players, notably Richter, have talked about wanting to play winter ball in Mexico.

Shwam shakes his head.

"You've got legit Double-A and Triple-A guys who go there, not to mention your big-league guys who are on rehab or want to learn a new position. It's very hard for independent league guys to get a shot.

"Same way with the fall short-season leagues. They're affiliated-run. You have to be invited. I couldn't place one of our guys no matter how good he is."

So how can he help one of these kids after the season?

"Australia. I have connections. They play four games a week for two months. The travel is out the ass, but more and more it's getting to be a place where guys can be noticed."

Shwan says he has heard rumors that some Frontier League managers have bad-mouthed their star players to scouts to keep them from getting picked up.

"Easy to do. You've got a stud who's hit 15 home runs and carries the team on his shoulders. But you tell the Mets' cross-checker that he's a cancer in the clubhouse and the worst piece-of-shit human being you've ever seen. The scout moves on down the road and the guy stays in the lineup.

"That's so wrong it isn't even funny. What this league is about is to give kids a second chance. An affiliated team could come up to me with a grocery list. Let's see, we want Smuin, Fry and Brand. That would rip our team to shreds. We might not win another game. But I'd say, here they are, babe, right on a platter. It's simply the right thing to do."

Shwam wishes he could start the season with this group of players.

"The bad characters are gone. The ones who bail when the going got tough are gone. Weeding 'em out cost us some games, no question. Next time I won't bring in so many guys at training camp. We were too busy evaluating them baseball-wise to have any meaningful conversations about who they are as people. Gotta find out who's tough-minded and who doesn't love the game as much as he thinks he does. What's that word? Oh, yeah, profiling. Do some FBI shit."

AUGUST 21

Mark Thomas, the guy who almost didn't come to Evansville in May because he was afraid the team wouldn't be run in a professional manner, says the team hasn't been run in a professional manner.

"I'm not talking the bus rides so much. I know I bitched as much as anybody, but you've got to play through that. Twice this season, we got our paychecks late. There's no excuse for that. And we were forced to play on shitty fields with no regard for our safety. It's like we're a bunch of farm animals. Just go out there and plow."

What about Shwam?

"Oh, he's all right. He managed the way he has been successful in the past. I could play for him again. It was mostly the younger guys who had trouble with him."

Gateway beats the Otters, 6-1.

Carmichael: "This ain't the end, but the whipping stick is on the table."

Bill Bussing is disappointed in the attendance. Many games in the inaugural 1995 season drew more than 5,000 people. The crowds have slumped to an average of approximately 1,200, despite a much-increased marketing budget and the fact the man and his wife have scrubbed everything except the foul poles.

"We didn't create enough of a compelling entertainment experience," Bussing says. "We need more bubble machines out front, more roving musicians, clowns, that sort of thing. Sad to say, you can't package baseball as just sport any more."

He says the team will lose more than $100,000 this season.

"The Otters aren't an easy sell. Because we're not affiliated, it's like we're nobody's team. Too many of the players are anonymous. They come and go and there's not much in the way of name recognition. We need to get these kids out in the community. Let them speak at schools and club meetings. Show people that they're absolute princes."

AUGUST 22

Thomas, Adams and Harrison are assigned to early work. They meet with Todd Brown at the batting cage.

It is a completely different Adams than the guy who blew off pre-game a few days earlier.

He's focused. Engaged. Asking for help. Even giving it.

"You're not seeing the low, outside pitch," he tells Thomas. "Turn your hips. Drive your feet."

Adams demonstrates.

Thomas nods.

Evansville gives up seven runs in the fifth inning and goes down, 9-4. Harrison boots a double-play ball at third that would have ended the inning. Some fans boo. Harrison, shaken, apologizes to everybody in the dugout.

Carmona and Nerei hit solo home runs. Fry takes the loss.

The Otters are six games behind division-leading Dubois with seven to play.

Carmichael: "This is like getting stirred in a shitpot."

Shwam says he'll change his approach to managing if he comes back to Evansville next summer.

"I'll treat it more like a college situation. Be more approachable. You don't have to pound something in my head for me to learn. These are younger guys. Compared to the Northern League, they're like little kids. I have to bring everything down to that level."

No more hard-ass?

"Doesn't work. I know that now. You've got to set yourself up as their buddy. Shit, some managers in this league go out and drink beer with their players. I'm not talking about on the bus after a game, but in clubs. Sit together like it's old home week."

Shwam shakes his head.

"I can't see that. You lose that line of respect. If they see you out on the dance floor making an ass of yourself, how can you release them the next day? You pull that shit in affiliated ball and you're fired in a heartbeat.

"But I can change. I'm not that old. I can play Walt Disney with the best of them. I can get my players to say, 'Hey, Shwamie is a good guy.' But I'll say this. The first day of coddling is the end of the line as far as being signed by an affiliated team. I'll do it like Greg Tagert. Have a happy-go-lucky clubhouse. Tell the kids this is the last place they're ever going to play ball. Screw getting picked up. Just enjoy each other's company and play the season."

AUGUST 23

Mattingly gives the signal for a curve. He gets a heater. The ball bounces off his glove toward the dugout. He falls down the steps and hits his head on the concrete floor. He finishes the inning, but tells Becka he is seeing double and having trouble breathing. The ambulance takes him to the emergency room.

Top of the ninth. Score tied at 2. River City has runners on first and second. Base hit to Cosbey in left. The runner is waved around third. Cosbey's strong throw arrives in time, but backup catcher Al Ready doesn't make the tag. Otters fall, 3-2.

Dubois wins. Evansville can forget the post-season.

AUGUST 25

Becka says Mattingly has a concussion. Nothing serious, but he's done for the year.

"I don't know what it is about me taking people to the hospital, but it seems like it always takes forever," she says. "An hour goes by and I'm still sitting there, holding Brandon's head. Then the paramedics come. I think, great, maybe we can get out of here sometime tonight. They tell me they were told the call was for a 65-year-old man with a stroke. I told them Mattingly will probably have that happen to him one of these days, but, for now, it's a blow to the head.

"I guess they just thought he was another scruffy ballplayer. Nobody stabilized his neck and back. They handled the poor guy like he was a bag of potatoes. Definitely not what I learned in school."

The Otters win their home finale, 5-2, over River City. Miller only yields one earned run in seven innings and finishes the year with a 9-5 record.

Richter is brought in to pitch the ninth, but leaves the game in pain after facing only one hitter.

"This is the first time dating back to Little League that I wasn't able to throw a ball as hard as I could," Richter says after the game. "My elbow started hurting four days ago. I hoped that some rest would help, but it didn't. I had absolutely nothing out there.

"I'm hoping it's not injured, only hurting. It would be very hard on me if a bone spur or torn tendon ends my pitching career with so many questions unanswered. I still don't know how good I could be and I really want to find out.

"I know it has been a long season and we haven't been all that successful, but I'm not ready for it to be over. Bosse Field has been my home for the last few months. You bring into your heart so many things. The glow of the lights. The energy of the crowd. The nervousness of stepping on the rubber. The satisfaction of shaking hands after a win. I don't want to let them go. It will be emotional for me just to say goodbye to the batboys. I don't know how I can handle the guys I've played with for so long."

Richter says Tom Miller looked terrible before the game.

"I asked what was wrong and the guy broke down. He knew he was pitching his last game as a professional. He spent the entire day calling all the people who were responsible for him playing baseball and thanking them for their support. He said he was doing fine until he got to his dad and that is when he started crying.

"I realize this is the low-level minors, but it shows just how strongly some players feel about the game and how much it means to be a part of it. I was so proud of Tom for not being ashamed to admit his feelings. I've learned so much from him. When it's my turn to play my last game, he will be at the top of my list to call."

AUGUST 26

The Otters sweep a meaningless doubleheader at Dubois, 12-5 and 7-1. Coronado gets five hits. Harrison knocks in four runs. Nerei manages to avoid being hit by a pitch.

I ask Shwam to review the Otters' roster, a player at a time, with an eye on whether he would want them for the 2001 team, even though the manager isn't certain if he'll be back next year.

- Thomas: "Tough choice. Mark would be a true veteran and I can only have three. He would have to guarantee that he'll hit with more power."
- Cosbey: "I'd love to have him back, but he'll be too old. If he plays, it would only be with an affiliated team."
- Coronado: "I think he wanted me to rest him early in the year, and then he realized he'll never get out of this place unless he can prove he's an everyday player. He's one tired puppy right now and his bat speed has slowed. I'd take him back, though."
- Figueroa: "Our best pure hitter. I'd welcome him, too."
- Nerei: "He's done here."
- Adams: "He'd have a lot of convincing to do."
- Harrison: "The guy would have to get better on defense and he'd have to be able to hit more home runs."
- Mattingly: "I think he's done all he can do at this level."
- Smuin: "He'll be on an affiliated team."
- Love: "I don't think so."
- Stelzner: "He wants to be a starter. I don't see him as one."

- Honda: "I hope he comes back."
- Ready: "I would invite him to camp."
- Richter: "For sure. I think he needs another full season at this level."
- Blaylock: "Too immature on the mound. Gets rattled when he gets lit up. Next year he wouldn't be the mop-up guy. He'd have to put up some numbers."
- Law: "I don't think so. If I bring him back, I'd need another shortstop because Keith gets dinged so much."
- Carmona: "I would be willing to evaluate him next year."
- Delgado: "He wants to go affiliated, but he's only been an everyday player for part of one season. He would benefit from another year here."
- Carmichael: "At first, he was hesitant to make a decision. I was coaching him. He's better now. More forceful. I could work with him again."

As for anybody he cut in training camp or during the season, Shwam says, "No. I don't believe in recycling."

AUGUST 27

Before the game, Nerei and Honda have an animated conversation in Japanese. A few butts down, Figueroa and Delgado are carrying on in Spanish.

"This has definitely been a sociological experiment," Figueroa says. "I don't think there's any other sport where so many cultures come together. You don't have to study abroad. Just play for the Otters."

Mattingly says he will talk with Bill Bussing after the season.

"I'm gonna say, 'Look, here are some reasons why we lost. The bus was shit. You can't build team chemistry when you're always bringing in new players. Guys get stressed and they don't perform.' I know what Shwam says about worry about yourself, but it's a team game. You have to feed off each other. Dan was pretty cool by the end of the year, but at first there wasn't enough leadership from him. Not enough talk. Most of the time, the game wasn't fun this year."

Smuin walks six and throws four wild pitches in the 6-1 setback.

Dubois, which is in danger of losing its franchise, draws only 453 fans.

Becka says her perspective has changed a lot over the summer.

"For a while, I wanted the season to be over so bad, but then I got to know them as people instead of ballplayers. The first time I took Thomas to the doctor, I was a little scared because I was convinced he's a crazy person. But he has a great sense of humor and I enjoy being around him.

"And Mattingly. Early in the year, every time his name would come up I'm like, oh, God, get him away from me. But he's really a very intuitive guy. On one road trip, he must've spent an hour asking how I was doing and stuff.

"We were on the bus the other night and my name came up and everybody sang 'My Girl.' Shwam even had a solo. It was very sweet."

AUGUST 28

The Otters board the bus for the last game of the year, take their seats and think back over the season.

Mattingly playing pepper with little kids in front of the dugout.

Hudson putting White-Out on his fingers like he has seen big-league catchers do so their signs can be more easily seen by their pitchers.

Cosbey's white shoes and black bat.

The nightly ritual of Harrison asking Becka to put his snuff in her jacket.

Coronado explaining that the reason he stole second base so easily was because the catcher put down three fingers and he knew he could outrun any off-speed pitch.

Suraci needing to take a piss during a 30-minute inning, jumping the fence to go to the shed of a bathroom only to see a dozen guys ahead of him and returning to his position and managing to hold his water until after the third out.

Harrison dropping his drawers to show the seamer on his ass where he got hit by a pitch.

Richter telling me the greatest thing about baseball is that, in the end, everything returns to how it should be.

In the dugout, the Otters looks more like tourists than players. Most have cameras. Several are passing balls around to be signed.

There's a 12-inch rip in the seat of Coronado's pants. Other uniforms are mangled, but Jeremy's is the only one that looks like it has been in a knife fight.

I tell him I've heard of the Lord moving in mysterious ways, but never through flapping fabric.

"The Lord is still moving," he explains. "I just can't sew."

The players are more relaxed than if this was a neighborhood softball game.

It shows in their performance, possibly the best of the year.

Shortstop Law makes a great play on a line drive.

Thomas crashes into the fence to bring down a deep fly.

Figueroa gets three hits and steals two bases.

"I told myself that I gotta get me at least one bag before the season's over," he says. "I mean, I'm Latin, right? Good baserunners, right? I can't let my people down."

Coronado and Law execute a perfect double steal from third and first.

Honda pitches six shutout innings.

Cosbie beats out another bunt.

Miller gets a hotfoot.

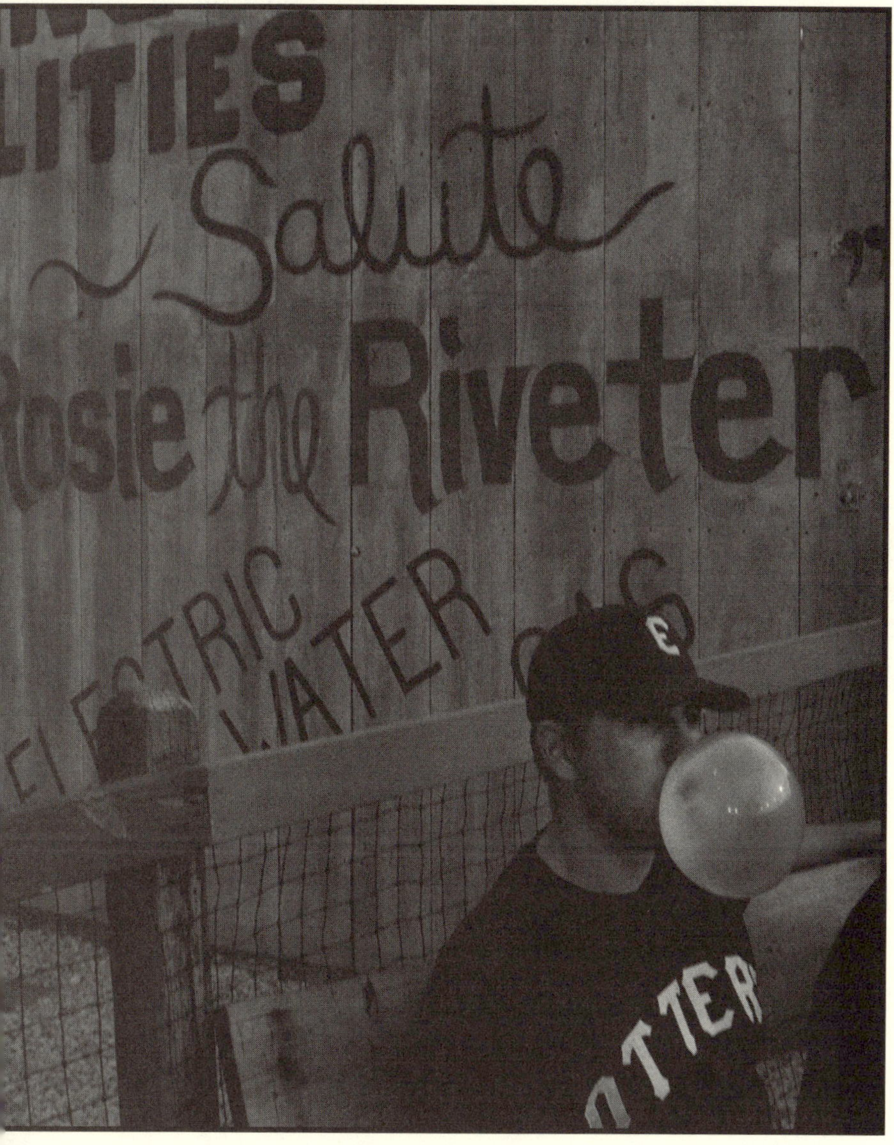
LITIES
Salute
osie the Riveter
ECTRIC
WATER

The Otters win, 7-1.

Shwam embraces each player as he comes off the field. Not just parting pats. Full hugs.

The kids give as good as they get.

"Thanks, Dan," several say.

"Shit, thank you," the skip replies.

Shwam calls his last team meeting.

"We were coming together as a squad. That's a fact. I believe we're the best team in the league. We should be in the playoffs. Shit, we ought to show up at the first post-season game. Dressed and ready to play. Just to see what they'd do.

"Take a good look around. You're never gonna see a lot of these people again. As close as we've been for three months, we're gonna be that far away. I hope to God that baseball continues for each man here. Some of you didn't like some of the things I did this season. I know I made mistakes. Shit, I'm not Joe Torre. But don't let anything I did keep you from coming back to the game. We can all look each other in the eye and know we went at it as hard as we could."

The players engage in one last round of picture-taking before gathering their gear and heading for the bus. They're laughing and joking. Hats are turned backwards. Gloves are on top of heads. Shirttails are out. Socks are pulled down.

Mark Thomas stands alone on the third-base line and stares at the field.

Several minutes pass. Thomas doesn't move.

"What's he looking at?" a fan wonders aloud. "Game's over. Nothing to see."

Thomas ignores him and continues his vigil. He adjusts his uniform on the off chance that the league commissioner will decree another nine innings.

"Guy's nuts," the fan says, stacking his beer cups and turning to go.

For all Thomas knows, he has played in his last game. Gotten his last rip. Thrown his last pipe.

The grounds crew rakes home plate and pulls the tarp over the pitcher's mound.

The stadium lights begin to dim.

No word from the commish. Must be out of the office.

Thomas walks soldier-like to the gate. Hat and glove where they should be.

Professional.

Full of grace, he leaves.

Wishing it didn't have to be over.

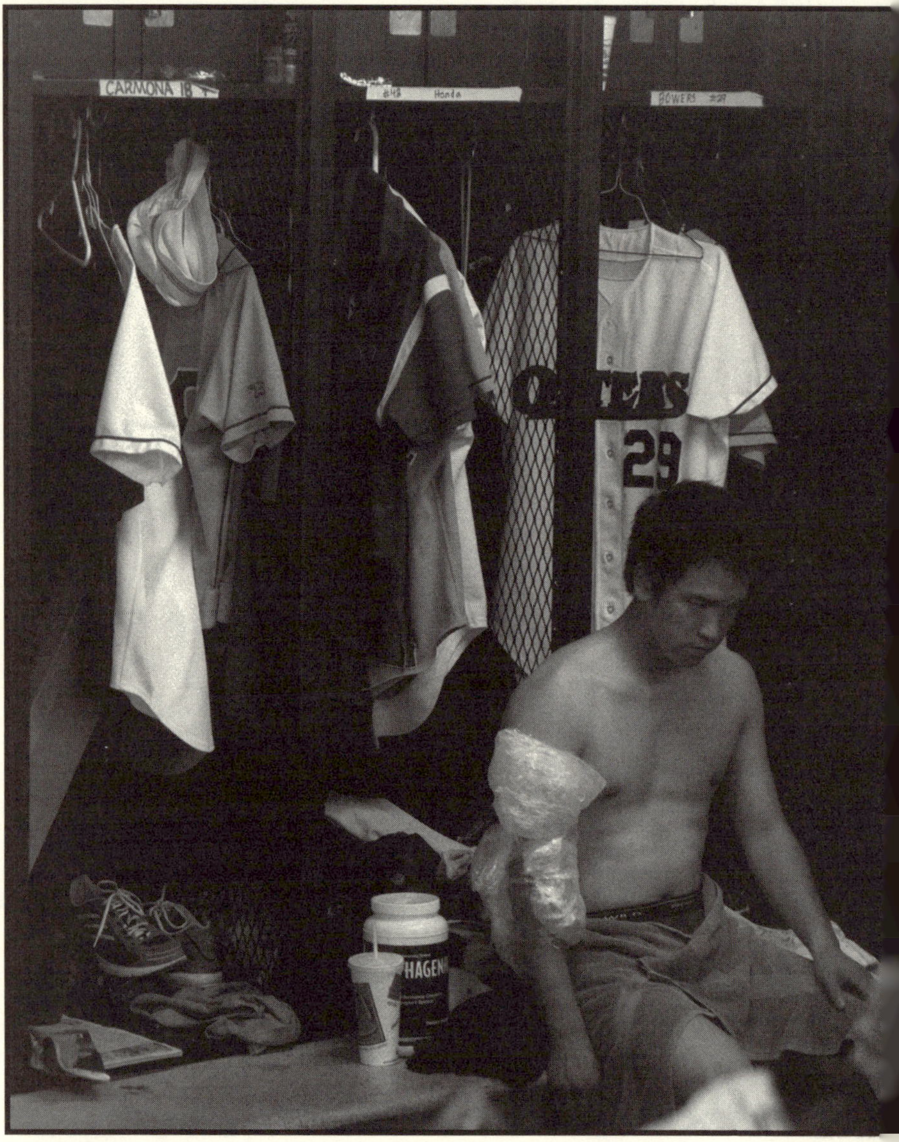
CARMONA 18
Honda
BOWERS
29

Epilogue

THREE MONTHS AFTER the last game, Mark Shuster announced Dan Shwam will not be back for the 2002 season. The skip, who says he didn't hear jackshit from the Otters' organization, will manage the Tyler, Texas, Roughnecks of the independent All-American Association.

Cosbey is named MVP. He hit .295 and stole 38 bases.

Bill Murray never showed up.

Thomas batted .266.

Figueroa's late surge earned him the team batting title with a .366 mark. Coronado finished at .354.

Richmond won the league title over Dubois.

Smuin struck out 100 in 80 innings.

Lisa Rust received a flower arrangement from Cosbey's mother. The card contained $300 and a note thanking her for taking such good care of Chris.

It took two days and four trash bags for Lisa Rust to clean up the room used by her summer sons.

Honda finished his English reader and, by the end of the year, could occasionally understand Mattingly.

Law's average dropped to .245. If he had lost any more weight, he would have needed an air bag to keep his uniform from falling down.

Shwam got thrown out of three games. Thomas led the players with two ejections.

Nerei hit 10 home runs in 44 games.

Harrison ended the season at .273, but topped the team in knuckle salutes. He says, "It would not be a defeat to be an Otter again, but I'd have to be playing."

Becka never did find a host family. She met a nanny and moved in with her.

She was hired by Jacksonville (Fla.) University as an athletic trainer. Because the baseball season stretches into June, she doubts she'll come back to the Otters for the 2002 season.

Mattingly was hired by the sheriff's department. He says he won't play any more.

Law says he will hire a personal trainer and intensify his workouts in the hope a contact back home can get him individual tryouts with affiliated teams. If nothing works out, he would play another season for the Otters.

Stelzner is "90 percent sure" he won't return. He says he wants to see another part of the country.

Carmichael and Ryan hope to be back.

Smuin will work construction over the winter. If he gets a call from an affiliated team, he'll start throwing.

Blaylock would re-enlist with the Otters.

So would Fry.

Love will ask Shwam to find him a job.

Delgado says if no other teams call, he will consider a second season in Evansville.

Cosbey's doctor in California told him physical therapy two times a week for six weeks will get his elbow ready for next season. He says a fall tryout with San Diego went well and there is a "strong possibility" he will either be signed or invited to spring training in 2002.

Thomas would like to play in the Northern League next season.

So would Todd Brown.

Coronado made peace with Lisa Rust's dogs.

INNING
P TEAM 1 2 3 4 5 6 7 8 9 10 11 R H E
Visitors
STRIKES BALLS OUTS
BR Associates, Inc.
Wendy's
READ ABOUT THE Rockford Peaches IN THE MORNING STAR
Coca-Cola
DAYS INN
OTTERS